PRAISE FOR SHERRY RICHERT BELUL'S
SAY IT NOW

"Sherry is the central switchboard of kindness, a pure light source. She seems to be everywhere at once with more attention beamed on everything than most people can even imagine. How does she do it? My introduction to Sherry was via a letter of appreciation she sent me for my poetry, but she's a living example of all that she teaches about expressing love and appreciation to everyone in every way we can. In a world that often feels too full of violence, fear, and anger, we need all the kindness we can get. Sherry's work sparks courage in ways that create contagious light. And those tiny lights beam out into the world, changing hearts and moods and minds."

—Naomi Shihab Nye, Poet and author of *The Red Suitcase*

"Brendon and I have both received books from Sherry filled with loving and positive quotes from people in our community. These books literally make you cry happy tears; they are filled with so much joy. Sherry is a blessing to everyone around her, and she reminds us all to do something for people in our lives to say I see you, I appreciate you, keep going. You never know when someone around you needs a boost. Sherry's work will inspire you to share gratitude, love, and appreciation in new creative ways."

—Denise & Brendon Burchard, The Burchard Group/HPX Life

"The Celebration Book created by Simply Celebrate was by far the most beautiful gift I've ever received. A magnificent surprise! I literally sobbed when I read it. Wow, what a keepsake! Sherry's work is an example of the power of appreciation and celebration. I'm glad she's out there encouraging this kind of expression of joy!"
—Marcia Wieder, CEO and founder of Dream University

"Sherry Richert Belul's work helps jumpstart joy for anyone who feels stuck or not enough. Sherry shares pinpoints of light to move people away from inner shadows toward happiness and celebration. She offers an exciting voice of hope, love, and compassion."
—Randy Taran, founder of Project Happiness

"Sherry Richert Belul showed up to Life is a Verb Camp with a bag full of magic, creating joy, connection, and happiness in amazing and beautifully simple ways. The Mailbags o' Love she created facilitated so much appreciation and celebration that we awarded Sherry the event 'VIP: Golden Heart' Award and have made those mailbags a new tradition. I can't imagine ever having camp without her Joy Ninja self again!"
—Patti Digh, Founder, Life is a Verb Camp and author, *Life is a Verb*

"I head up a company dedicated to building relationships between coaches, authors, and entrepreneurs, so I know the power of bringing appreciation, joy, and celebration into our relationships in new and daring ways. Sherry Richert Belul brings her own brand of joy and celebration to our members in the form of warmth, high energy, unfailing encouragements, and simple joy. Her appreciation and celebration practices have landed on my own doorsteps numerous times and always astound me with impeccable timing and personalized care."

—Rich German, author of *Monetize Your Passion* and founder of Joint Venture Insider Circle

"Sherry Richert Belul is part street urchin, part Mary Poppins. Like magic, she shows up in unexpected places—sometimes in the mess of despair or depression, miraculously in the moment we need it—to remind us all of the power of appreciation and love."

—Susan Harrow, author of *Sell Yourself Without Selling Your Soul* and CEO of prsecrets.com

"Working with Sherry to create a Celebration Book was an absolute joy, and the final product is nothing short of spectacular. My wife loves her gift, and this incredible keepsake will be a treasure for us to enjoy for a lifetime!"

—Steve Olsher, New York Times bestselling author of *What Is Your WHAT?* and host of Reinvention Radio

"As a recipient of one of Sherry's celebration books, I can attest to the deep, soulful impact of these books. Sherry is a happiness Ninja, someone who has an infectious energy and amazing skill at making people feel elevated, inspired, and that they are part of a community of other inspirationalists. Her life's work has been built on the premise of 'turning ordinary moments into an extraordinary life,' and she offers countless ways for others to find all of the 'pinpricks of light' in their own lives."

—Maya Stein, founder of The Creativity Caravan, author of *Writing Prompts for Ordinary People*, Brave Girls University teacher

"Sherry Belul's caring and fun attitude is contagious, her message clear and inspiring. Her exercises for deep learning took us deep quickly. No wonder when I asked new members what they wanted in speakers, the first two answers were 'More like her!' "

—Pat McHenry Sullivan, program director, East Bay Women's Network

"On a recent long plane ride, I pressed 'random play' on my audios, and what really stood out to me was so many amazing recordings in which Sherry's voice was shining through with positivity, enthusiasm, bouncy joyful high spirits...and oodles of perfectly-crafted encouragements. It was so moving and encouraging! I'm just one of the many people Sherry's infectious high spirits have bolstered. The truth is that you never know when something you said to someone is being remembered and replayed and is making a huge difference in their lives, like Sherry's amazing recordings did for me. Sherry teaches us all the ripple effects of love."

—Rob Witig, founder of Netprov Studio and Sherry's coaching client

"I love the idea of these creative one-of-a-kind gifts. Last year I downloaded Sherry's printable Love List, wrote on it by hand, and mailed it to my mother-in-law. She cried! A good cry! She told everyone that it was the best gift she could have received. I did the same for friends' birthdays this year, and one friend said that no one had EVER told her things that they loved about her. A friend is having surgery today for cancer, and it dawned on me this morning to create a Joy Jar for her after I watched Sherry's video from the email she sent out!! I'm sure this loving gift will help my friend recover. All of the creativity brought by Sherry is so refreshing and so needed. Sherry's work is powerful beyond measure."

—Melissa Brown, Simply Celebrate reader

Published by The Tiny Press, an imprint of Mango Publishing Group, a division of Mango Media Inc.

Cover: © Joanna Price, www.joannapricedesign.com
Layout & Design: Morgane Leoni

For permission requests, please contact the publisher at:

Mango Publishing Group
2850 Douglas Road, 2nd Floor
Coral Gables, FL 33134 U.S.A.
info@mango.bz

For special orders, quantity sales, course adoptions and corporate sales, please email the publisher at sales@mango.bz. For trade and wholesale sales, please contact Ingram Publisher Services at customer.service@ingramcontent.com or +1.800.509.4887.

Say It Now: 33 Ways to Say "I Love You" to the Most Important People in Your Life

Library of Congress Cataloging-in-Publication number: 2019935682
ISBN: (print) 978-1-64250-035-6, (ebook) 978-1-64250-036-3
BISAC category code REF019000 REFERENCE / Quotations

Printed in the United States of America.

Say it Now

Say it Now

33 creative ways to say I LOVE YOU
to the most important people in your life

Sherry Richert Belul

Founder of Simply Celebrate

the
tiny
press

For my mother, Rebecca, who always seeks the light and gives
more generously than anyone I know.

CONTENTS

FOREWORD BY ALEXANDRA FRANZEN

The first time I met Sherry, she was wearing one of her signature knit hats, purple fingerless gloves, and a beaming smile. With her small frame and sparkling eyes, she looked like a woodland fairy—possibly hiding a pair of wings under that coat.

We were at a writing center in the Bay Area of California. Miniature muffins, mixed nuts, coffee, and tea were being laid out on a long table. Fellow writers milled around, snacking and chatting about their current projects. Sherry and I found a quiet corner of the room and I asked about her work.

"I heard you run a business," I mentioned. "What type of work do you do?"

"I help people celebrate everyday life," Sherry told me.

She told me about her company—Simply Celebrate—and her mission, which is to remind people to say "I love you" to the ones they cherish most. Not just on special occasions, like birthdays and anniversaries, but every single day.

She told me about some of the products she offers, like Tribute Books filled with heartfelt messages and photos for a special person in your life, and classes on creative gift-making, letter-writing, and more.

She also told me about her past struggles with depression. During the darkest chapter of her life, when it was difficult to get out of bed and function at the most basic level, Sherry discovered that simple things—like taking a few moments to write a letter to a friend—helped her to feel the tiniest little spark of optimism. Through her own experiences, Sherry learned that when you send a little love toward someone else—toward a friend, a parent, a teacher, anyone who's important to you—they're usually surprised and delighted and it really makes their day. But it makes your day, too. You feel lighter, brighter, a little more hopeful about the future, all because of the small moment of connection you've shared with another human being.

"Pinpricks of light," Sherry calls it. Every time you text a friend to say, "You're amazing," every time you write a list of "reasons why I love you" and mail it to your sister, every time you bring a small gift to a colleague at work, show up for a friend who needs a lift to the hospital, or lend a helping hand, it creates a little spark of light in their day—and in yours, too.

Over the next several years, Sherry and I kept in touch through emails and occasional video and audio messages. One day, Sherry emailed me and told me she was ready to start writing her next book.

"What's the title?" I asked.

"*Say It Now*," she told me.

She went on to explain her vision for the book.

She told me, "At people's funerals, everyone gathers around and says all these beautiful things about the person who just died—how precious they were, how kind and smart, how creative and generous, how much they were appreciated, and all the reasons why. I always think, why do we wait until someone's dead to express how much we love them? Why aren't we saying these words—to their face—while they're alive? Why not say it now? Imagine how wonderful that would be!"

I was struck by the simplicity and power of this message. It's so true. We human beings tend to pound on through life in a busy, dizzy blur. We rarely take five seconds to say, "Thank you," or "You mean so much to me," or "Let me tell you why you're amazing!" We rarely look up from our phones long enough to make eye contact and exchange a few kind words with the person standing right there, just two feet away. We wait until it's too late—sometimes, until someone has passed away—before we realize our mistake.

There are Christians and Muslims and Buddhists. Sherry is, in her own words, a Celebrationist. She is one of those rare people who takes time, every single day of her life, to celebrate the people that she loves—and to celebrate the miracle of being alive. She doesn't just talk about it—she lives this message. It radiates from every inch of her being. She has inspired me to "say it now" in so many ways—writing postcards to friends, recording video messages for my clients, checking in with friends who are struggling with health issues, and taking a spontaneous trip to Tahiti with my mom instead of putting it off until "next year." My life has been enriched because of Sherry's influence.

I'm so glad that Sherry created this precious little book—the one you're about to read. It's filled with simple ideas on how to say "I love you" to the most important people in your life—your husband, wife, girlfriend, boyfriend, kids, parents, teachers, mentors, and other people who are meaningful to you, like perhaps a yoga teacher or the local librarian.

Whether you decide to express your feelings in the form of a letter, a list, a thoughtful gift, a surprise, a favor, a hug, or all of the above, I know this book will inspire you to stop waiting and say it now. As Sherry reminds us, the greatest gift you can give to another human being is the gift of a few moments of your undivided attention. And the right time for that type of gift is today...and every day...forever and always.

INTRODUCTION

Hello. I'm so glad you found your way to this book!

My name is Sherry. I run a company called Simply Celebrate.

Professionally speaking, I wear many hats—writer, teacher, artist. But essentially, I'm a professional gift maker. At Simply Celebrate, people hire me when they want to create a thoughtful gift for someone they love—like an audiogram filled with messages for Grandma, or a tribute book to honor Uncle Larry on his sixtieth birthday, or a Love List for Mother's Day (or any day of the year).

My life's work is helping people celebrate everyday life and the people they love.

When people hear what I do, most of the time, they think, "Oh, Sherry is one of those naturally happy people who bounds out of bed each morning. Creativity and joy probably come easily to her."

Nope. Not so.

The truth is, I have a history of anxiety and depression. My interest in gift-giving actually began during the darkest time of my life—a time when I was feeling like I didn't even want to be alive. I was struggling to find a reason to stay on this planet. I couldn't even imagine a life of joy.

Have you ever experienced anything like this?

It was 1991. I had just broken up with my boyfriend after a recent move to San Francisco. I was brokenhearted and grappling with a depression that had been nipping at my heels for years. I couldn't kick it off this time.

By luck, a friend of mine gifted me with a book by Zen teacher Cheri Huber. This book led me to take a meditation class. I still remember how I felt walking into that first class. I was in such a place of pain and darkness that it felt like an iron wall closing in on me. There was no relief.

The instructor had us focus on our breath. Breathing in. Breathing out. Breathing in. Breathing out. And a tiny miracle happened. I breathed in and I realized that—for just one brief moment, for one full breath—there was no pain. There was a moment of relief. A moment of peace. A moment of hope. Then I exhaled, and all the pain came rushing back, of course. But for that one brief moment, I saw a crack in the iron all around me. It was like a tiny pinprick of light.

The next day, I had a moment in which I saw a wide blue sky. I had a moment in which I lay in the sun and held my cat, feeling her purr. I tasted the blueberry jam on my toast. Each of these felt like more pinpricks of light in that iron wall. All of these moments helped me realize that I could consciously turn my attention to moments of joy instead of toward the pain.

After some time passed, I realized that I didn't have to wait for these moments to occur in my life. I could seek them out. I could create moments of well-being and joy.

To heal from depression, some people do yoga, some people do therapy, some people try medication, or all of the above. I started making gifts. It became a daily practice, like a form of meditation. These gifts were not fancy or complicated. Just a quick "thank you" note for a friend or family member, or a list of reasons "why I appreciate you so much." Each time I sent a little burst of gratitude toward someone, I felt that beautiful pinprick of light once again. A moment of celebration. A moment of joy. It's really no exaggeration to say that gift-giving saved my life.

This is the magical thing about creating a gift for someone in your life. Not only does it feel amazing to receive that kind of love, but it feels fantastic to give that kind of love, too. It's healing and uplifting for everyone involved.

I've spent the last twenty years exploring what it means to deliberately seek out joy and consciously create moments of appreciation and celebration. I've learned that joy doesn't just land on me; joy is a practice. And "celebration" isn't just something for special occasions, like birthdays or anniversaries. Celebration is a way of life.

So you can see why I'm so glad you're here.

This book is an invitation to create more joy and celebration for yourself—and for the people you love. It's all about saying what you feel and expressing your love—and doing it now.

AN INVITATION

Let's get started! Inside this book, you'll find thirty-three creative gift ideas. It's okay if you're not a particularly artsy or crafty person. Most of these gift ideas don't require any special skills. Just choose any gift idea that appeals to you. Try it out. In doing so, you'll create a moment of light for someone else—and for yourself, too.

I titled this book *Say It Now* because it's so important to express our feelings now—not someday later. Many people have a tendency to procrastinate and push things into the future. We think, "I'll plan a fun date night...next week." Or, "I'll call Mom to say hi...tomorrow." But life is brief and precious and full of unexpected (and sometimes tragic) twists of fate. Tomorrow might be one day too late.

So if there's something you want to say—"I love you," "I appreciate you," "Thank you for everything," "You amaze me," "I'm grateful we're friends"—I'm urging you to say it now, as soon as possible.

As you'll see throughout this book, you can "say it now" in a literal way—with a written note or a list of reasons why you love someone. Or you can "say it now" through your actions rather than your words— accompanying someone to their chemo appointment, for example, or showing up at their door with flowers.

Whether you're expressing yourself through your words, through your actions, or both, it doesn't matter. The point is to find a way to *say it* that feels right for you and the person you love.

Listen to what's in your heart about why you love this person— and say it.

I hope this book inspires you to celebrate life every day—with words, with cake, with sparklers, with music, with a tender moment spent with someone you love, or with sitting in silence and perhaps doing nothing at all.

To life!

Sherry

QR Code

Watch a two-minute video where I introduce myself ("Hello!") and share my Celebration Manifesto.

simplycelebrate.net/hello

HOW TO USE THIS BOOK

You may have purchased this book because you have a big occasion coming up and you want to give an amazing gift. Maybe your mom is turning seventy, your best friend is having his fortieth birthday, or it is your tenth wedding anniversary. Maybe you'd like to do something extra special to mark this milestone.

Maybe you have a friend who has cancer and is going through chemo and you want to show her how much you love and support her during this difficult time.

Maybe you're in a long-distance relationship and you want to send your sweetheart a series of gifts in the mail.

Perhaps you don't need a special gift for someone right now, but you love creative projects—and you love the idea of spreading joy through the art of gifting.

These are all great reasons to use this book.

Here are two ways you can dive in right now:

- Start reading at the beginning and use Post-it Notes to mark the gift ideas you know you want to try. Let your intuition guide you. Trust any small sparks of excitement you feel. If you get an idea for someone specific to give that gift to, write his or her name on the Post-it Note on that page.
- Open the book up at a random page or simply skim through the pages, letting your creativity guide you. If a description or photo grabs your attention, stop and read more. Use your Post-it Notes here, too, to mark any gift ideas that seem fun to you.

Something important to keep in mind:

As you are reading the ideas in this book, you'll want to use your imagination to think about how these ideas could be converted or tweaked for different ages or types of people. These ideas are great as is, but they are even better when you add your own special flavor of love and thoughtfulness.

Ask yourself these questions as you go:

- Could I make this gift work for someone who is elderly or for a small child? What would I need to change in order for that to happen?
- Could I make this gift even more personal or special? How?
- What could I incorporate into this gift that would show the recipient that I really see, know, and love who she is?
- Is there some humorous twist I could include to make him laugh?
- Is there a way to present this gift to make it the most fun, comfortable, and/or enjoyable?

HOW TO USE THE QR CODES IN THIS BOOK

You'll notice a bunch of squares with squiggly lines in them throughout the book. These are called Quick Response or QR codes. Many of you are familiar with these QR codes. Some of you may not be. That's okay!

QR codes are just barcodes that you can scan easily using an app on your smartphone. (If your eyes are glazing over right now, just skip the QR codes altogether and know that you can simply type in the URL that is also included. Easy-peasy!)

If, like me, you find QR codes to be kind of fun, like treasure hunts, you can try it here! See the squiggly square on the next page? I created this special code just for you to test this whole thing out.

How to scan the QR code if you have a smartphone older than 2018:

Step 1: Download a free QR code reader onto your smartphone by searching the App Store. (I use QR Reader, but, honestly, I don't remember how or why I chose that one.)

Step 2: Tap the app once it has downloaded to your phone in order to open the QR Reader. Tap again, and your camera will appear to be on. Hover over the code on this page, and the camera will automatically take a picture of the QR code. You'll be directed to the web page with my video message for you.

It's a fun way for me to get to share way more resources with you than I could squeeze in this book. It also allows me to show you videos and share audio recordings.

Note: Many newer smartphones have included QR code scanning that works by simply using the camera, without the necessity for the QR code reader app. If your smartphone has this feature, simply frame the QR code with your camera and it will launch into action.

But again, if you are shrugging your shoulders and rolling your eyes at the thought of this technology elbowing its way into your book, you can skip the extra resources altogether or simply type in any URL beneath the QR code.

QR Code

I created a surprise for you so you could test out how to use this QR code, or if you prefer, you can see it by simply typing in the URL.

simplycelebrate.net/surprise

WHY BOTHER MAKING A SPECIAL, PERSONAL GIFT?

Why Not Just Buy Something at the Store?

If you wanted to create a sweet moment for someone you love, you could send an electronic gift card. You could send a text filled with cute emojis. You could send a gift that you purchased on Amazon.

There's nothing wrong with any of those options, of course. Texts can be great. Amazon is definitely very efficient. However, if you want to make an extra-special impact in your recipient's day, I'd encourage you to send a gift that feels...different, something that's creative, personalized, and made with love; in other words, the type of gift you'll see inside this book!

Why bother giving this kind of gift? There are so many reasons:

- To have a deeper impact. A creative gift—like the ones in this book—can make your recipient feel seen, loved, understood, and appreciated.
- It's just more enjoyable. These kinds of gifts are so much fun to make. You'll love the creative process! Creating is much more enjoyable than schlepping around a shopping mall or exhausting yourself visiting online stores!
- Generate creative sparks. These kinds of gifts help you practice having fun and using your imagination in new ways.

- Create and nourish a real sense of connection. In our hyper-digital age, these kinds of gifts help people feel more human and less disconnected.

- Improve relationships. When you give these kinds of gifts, you'll be seen as someone who is creative, generous, and thoughtful—someone who goes the extra mile.

- Produce less waste and clutter. These kinds of gifts often cause less clutter. (Marie Kondo will be proud!)

- Spend less money. In this book, you'll find many creative gift ideas that cost very little, or practically nothing at all.

- Become a role model. If you give these kinds of gifts, you will inspire other people to give unconventional and fun gifts, too. You're modeling joy!

"But I'm Just Not Very Creative or Artistic... And Besides, I Don't Have Much Free Time."

We're just a few pages into this book, and you might already be having some doubts about all of this. Maybe you're thinking, "All of this sounds great—in theory—but I'm not an artistic or crafty person. I probably can't make any of the gifts in this book." Or maybe you're thinking, "I don't have time for this sort of thing." Or maybe there's some other type of hesitation creeping into your mind.

This is completely normal. I often feel this way, too. Whenever I step outside of my typical routine and try something new, there's always pushback from my Monkey Mind—or what my son calls "Squawky Polly." Squawky Polly is the part of my brain that gets all ruffled up when I start to experiment, take risks, or step more fully into the life I want to lead.

Scientists call Squawky Polly the "Reptilian Brain." It's the portion of our brain that exists to protect us from all the dangers of the world. As human beings, since we no longer face daily threats from bears or saber-toothed tigers, our brain finds other things to warn us about: Don't stand out or no one will like you. Don't expose yourself by being too open. Don't draw attention to yourself. Don't risk it. Don't be too loving, or people will think you are weird.

Making creative, loving gifts for people may not seem like something to be afraid of, but trust me.... your brain may try to stop you! Your job is to simply nod pleasantly in its direction, give a little wave, and continue on your path.

Here are three of ol' Squawky Polly's favorite excuses to stop you from actually putting this book into action:

"I don't have time for this."

Some of the gift ideas in this book will literally take you less than ten minutes to do. No kidding. I've intentionally included ideas that take little time but have a big impact. And even if you do choose a gift that takes an hour or two to create, you need to remember that the process of creating the gift is a gift to yourself.

Having the ability to use our imaginations and to create something out of nothing is one of the most exciting things about being a human. It is enlivening. It is fun. It will help you learn new things about who you are and how you are. You'll begin to notice strange synchronicities, and ideas will pop in out of nowhere. Let me repeat: this is fun. You have time for this because you are someone who will dedicate time to it because you value relationships, including your relationship with yourself and your creative life.

"I'm not creative."

Bah. Everyone is creative. It's just who and how we are. We are wired to connect the dots around us, to be sparked by things we see or hear, to imagine new things, to create new things.

Every day, in a thousand ways, we are creating. It's just that we may not always be conscious or intentional about it. When you think about what you want to have for dinner, and then you go get the ingredients and cook that dinner, you are creating. You might add in chili flakes or avocado because that sounds like it would be good. More creativity! You may be talking to a friend and suddenly get an idea about her soap business, and she's ecstatic. Maybe when you're dressing to go to the movie with your honey, you throw on that Italian scarf at the last minute, thinking it will add a little flair. These, my friend, are all creative moments.

There is no such thing as a person who is not creative.

"This feels too vulnerable."

You may set aside the time and look forward to using your creativity. Then ol' Squawky Polly whispers, "This feels too weird. Maybe it would be better to buy her a sweater." Don't believe it.

Yes, making a heartfelt gift might feel weird. That's okay. There is nothing wrong with weird. Just think of it as your heart pushing up against a wall, trying to grow a little bigger. It might feel uncomfortable, like something is wrong. But if you breathe into it and remind yourself that what you are doing is expanding the container for love, that might help.

Also, it is important to remember that we are living in a society that sometimes values safety over everything else. What if you were the person who stepped out of that safety zone in order to live a life that feels more vital and Technicolor? What if you inspired others to do so by your own courage?

Believe me, this is worth the feeling of vulnerability.

HOW TO PRESENT YOUR GIFT ONCE IT'S READY

"Once I've created my special letter or gift, how should I 'present' it to my mom or dad or friend or special someone? Should I just hand it to them? Hide it in their room? Mail it? What should I doooo?"

This is a surprisingly common question that lots of folks ask me! Here are my tips:

Wrapping

You've gone to a lot of effort to think of and create a unique gift. I hope you'll spend just a wee bit more time thinking about how to present the gift in a thoughtful way!

Presentation is important in that it kind of sets the tone for the gift receiver. It's like when you decorate a room for a party or add flourishes to a cake. It says, "Hey, something special is happening here; don't miss it!" It sets an anticipatory tone of delight.

So if your gift is something tangible, please don't wrap your well-thought-out gift in wrinkled brown paper or regifted tissue paper. Make it as special as the gift.

Wrapping doesn't have to be expensive. Be creative by visiting craft or thrift stores and seeing what fun finds can house your next gifts.

Let the presentation of your gift be a part of the gift, not an afterthought!

Timing

Consider the timing of your gift. Even the best gift in the world won't be well received if she's given it while she's in the middle of cooking dinner for twelve people or while you're in a loud, crowded place.

Make sure the recipient is able to fully focus on your gift. If it is ultra-personal, consider whether this is something you want to present with a lot of other people around or if it would be better one-on-one.

You can give the recipient a heads-up by saying something like, "I wanted to give you this during your party, but feel free to wait and read it later when you're alone." Or, "Hey, wanted you to have this now, but it might make your mascara run when you cry from joy, so I won't be offended it you wait and open it later!"

What If They Don't Like It?

You've created an amazing this-is-the-best-gift-ever kind of gift. You've presented it in a way that suits the person you are gifting and that gives the perfect weight and significance to the gift.

What if the unimaginable happens?

What if they don't like it?

If you are old enough to be reading this book, then you are likely old enough to know that there are never any guarantees in life. It's just the way it is. We could pour all our love and creativity into the perfect gift for someone, and yet when they open it, their face falls.

Whaaaaat? You might be thinking, "No way am I going to risk that," as you reach for the Crate & Barrel catalog on your desk.

32

Listen, one of my favorite things is to remember is that a gift or a present is an item given to someone without the expectation of payment or return.

If we're giving gifts, we are not expecting anything in return. And that includes gushing gratitude, happy exclamations, big hugs, or gosh-this-is-the-best-gift-evers.

But wait. Don't throw this book down and walk away muttering just yet.

In my experience, 99 percent of the time these kinds of gifts *are* received with gushing exclamations, tears of joy, and "I-can't-believe-you-did-this-for-me's." I could tell you hundreds and hundreds of stories about how these gifts have been the absolute perfect thing at the perfect time. I could tell you stories of oceans of happy tears. I can tell you about relationships that have been healed because of these kinds of say-it-now gifts. I could tell you of all the times someone has given a loving gift like this and it has meant the world to their loved one—and then that loved one has then unexpectedly died soon after, making it even more meaningful.

But, every once in a while, there might be something going on for the gift recipient that keeps her from receiving or loving your gift.

Here's an example. When I first met my beau, Ian, we went to out to hear some live music together. It was Gypsy Jazz, flavored with swing. Couples were dancing all around us. I confessed to Ian that I'd always wanted to learn how to dance but that I was too clumsy, all left feet.

Ian offered to take dance lessons with me. He was extraordinarily patient and really made an effort to make our lessons fun. I was thrilled that we were doing this together, but deep inside, I was also mortified every time we went to class. Ian has a natural talent for dance, and he is incredibly comfortable in his body. Having spent most of my earlier life trying to check out any way I could, I was disconnected from my body. Dancing was such a draw, but it was also foreign to me. I was in my head too much and not able to feel the music. It was very awkward!

I didn't let on to Ian the extent of this discomfort. Our relationship was still so new, and I longed to be the kind of woman I thought he deserved—and that was someone who was spontaneous and at ease in her body, not a forty-year-old woman who felt like she was a gawky nine-year-old.

Here's where that all met the moment of a perfect gift: one morning after I had spent the night at Ian's house, he and I walked to a nearby café to have breakfast. When we returned to his house, there was a surprise waiting for me. Ian had arranged for three musician friends to come to his house and play swing music for us in his apartment so we could dance.

He'd even had them set up some beautiful trays of food and wine for us. There were my favorite multicolored roses, the ones with half rose and half gold that look like sunsets. Everything was gorgeous. It was like I'd stepped into a movie.

Talk about romantic, right?

Yes. Except...

Except, I was the wrong person for the part. Instead of letting Ian swoop me up into his arms to dance gaily to the music they were playing, I slumped my shoulders and dragged my feet. Instead of being the leading lady, I turned into the self-conscious gawky nine-year-old. I was horrifyingly shy. My insides were all mixed up. I couldn't tell him what I was feeling because it was all happening so fast and I just felt like the absolute wrong person.

You see, Ian's gift was absolutely perfect. But at that moment, I wasn't able to receive it.

That gift happened twelve years ago. And what I want you to know is that I have now received that gift about a hundred times over. I got over my awkwardness about dancing and now Ian and I love to dance together. Whenever I think of that gift, I tell Ian how beautiful it was and how I wish I had been able to show up for it in the moment. I tell him how grateful I am and how much it warms my heart to think of his thoughtfulness and imagination. I want him to know that I've loved that gift so many times since he first gave it to me, but I wasn't able to love it right away (because I couldn't love me in that moment).

There are a couple things I want you to get from this story:

- Sometimes gifts are received days, weeks, months, or even years after we give them. Life is mysterious, and we can't know if or when our gift will have an impact.
- Sometimes people have to grow into their gifts, especially when they are gifts that are reflections of who that person is. We may be easily able to hold how awesome, unique, and lovable they are, but it might be a bit of a journey for them to accept all this goodness about themselves.
- We live in a world that is often focused on what's wrong and what's missing. It can be a useful practice for all of us—givers and receivers both—to be able to accept the joy of what is. It just might feel uncomfortable and way too vulnerable. That's okay.

- We might think we are giving one gift, but the person we love is receiving something else first. Like in my case, with Ian's beautiful surprise, what I received was a huge dose of self-knowledge, which led to an intention to do whatever it took to help myself become the leading lady in my own movie and to move past those outdated beliefs about myself.

- The purpose of a gift is about expressing joy, love, and creativity. It is about us putting love into action because that is what we're called to do. Ian had a blast planning that surprise for me. It made him so happy and he was allowing himself to fully express who he was. It is so key to remind ourselves a thousand times over that the payoff is in the moment of creating the gift. It is the love we generate by saying YES to who we want to be and how we want to show up.

Without further ado, let's get into some beautiful gift ideas! I'm so excited for you to choose one, create it, and give it to someone you love.

Let's Start Making Beautiful Things!

I want you to take a moment to appreciate yourself for being the sort of person who wants to live life with more celebration, joy, and connection.

I am so grateful for you. I've created a short video for you to help you celebrate who you are and your intention to give creative, conscious gifts!

QR Code

A video celebrating YOU, dear reader of
this book. Yup. YOU.

simplycelebrate.net/celebrating-you

"The fragrance always
stays in the hand
that gives the rose."

—Hadia Bejar

Remember, let yourself be the first recipient
of the joy of the gifts you give.

33 Ways to Say "I Love You" to the Most Important People in Your Life

Love lists, joy jars, treasure hunts,
toasts, tributes, celebration books,
quick surprises, audio and video messages,
thoughtful touches, acts of service...and more!

I Love You #1

THE LOVE LIST

"An extraordinary life is made up of extraordinary "moments"

Love list for Bella ...

- sweet
- snuggly
- silly
- sarcastic
- love to read
- comforting
- funny
- caring
- encouraging
- bright
- musical
- enthusiastic
- loving
- creative
- interesting
- enjoy reading tog
- talented in
- beautiful, bri, lla

- soft, milky cheeks
- fun to cook with
- like
- enjoy going out to eat together
- great hugs
- helped me be more patient
- you're sparkly
- beauti

The first gift idea I'd like to share with you is my all-time favorite. It's called the Love List—and it's simply a list of all the reasons why you love someone.

I love this gift because it's so simple to do, it costs nothing (or almost nothing) at all, it doesn't require any special arts and crafts skills, and it can be done in a tiny slice of time.

There are so many different types of Love Lists that you can create (I'm going to share many of my favorite options over the next several pages!) and so many fun ways to package and present your list once it's complete.

But before we get into the how-to instructions, I want to share a personal story with you. It's a story that shows why the simple act of writing down "reasons why I love you" can be so powerful for your recipient—and for you, too.

The Very First Love List I Ever Created

The very first Love List I ever made was in 1988. I was twenty-four years old, and my mom was turning fifty. I was just emerging from that selfish period that young people often go through—you know, when you don't really see your parents as real people with feelings, dreams, and needs outside of their relationship to you.

My mom raised me and my siblings all by herself. It was not an easy road. She worked long hours to make ends meet and was often exhausted when she came home from her job. I didn't really appreciate all of that when I was growing up. But with her fiftieth birthday approaching, I was reflecting on what an incredible woman she is, and I realized, "I don't think I've ever told my mom just how much I appreciate her."

For this milestone birthday, I wanted her to know that I saw her—That I really understood who she was as a person, how hard she worked, how much she sacrificed for her children, and everything she had created from so little.

I have no idea where the idea came from, but I remember thinking, "I'm going to make a list of fifty reasons why I love her."

I got a piece of paper and just started writing whatever came to mind.

- "You bake great cherry pie."
- "You taught me the value of books."
- "You are pleasant and cheerful to be around."
- "You are funny."
- "You are open-minded."
- "You listen."
- "You sew me drop-waist dresses by the dozens."
- "You always encouraged me to be whatever I want."

I just kept writing and writing without censoring or editing myself. Before I knew it, I had fifty things. And I kept going.

- "When I got a curly perm and hated it, you got one, too, so I wouldn't feel bad."
- "You were always the prettiest mom around: Sophia Loren, Jackie O, and Betty Boop all in one."
- "You let me make my own mistakes, and when I did, you'd always help me out."

- "You still love people even when they're not perfect—even when they're rude or mean, even when they hurt you."

My brain kept whirling out more, more, and more love, and pretty soon, I had a list of one hundred things.

I could have given my mom that handwritten list—and I'm sure she would have adored it. But I decided to make this Love List look and feel extra special. I bought some decorative stationery with hearts on it. Then I typed up my list on the avocado green Olivetti typewriter my mother had bought for me when I went away to college. I found a letter-sized envelope, tucked the list inside, sealed and stamped it, and mailed it off to my mom.

What I remember most about that day was the incredible *joy* that I felt. I remember practically skipping to the blue postal box at the corner of Fairfax and 3rd in Los Angeles where I was living at the time. I felt so *happy*.

After creating that list for my mom, something felt different inside me: more open, more alive. I felt like my heart had just grown a bit. (Remember the scene in *How the Grinch Stole Christmas!* when his heart grew three sizes? *Boink*! That's how I felt!) It was like all of this love and gratitude had been waiting inside of me all these years, just yearning for a chance to come out. And now, the treasure chest had been unlocked.

When my mom got that list of reasons why I love her, something shifted between us, too. Although I had always loved my mom, I'd never explicitly told her so. Or why. In all honesty, she'd often been an afterthought to my own self-centered world. But after she received that special birthday Love List, I could feel a difference in our connection.

It was like the invisible cord between us got a little bit stronger—like the tug was a little more palpable.

Making that Love List helped me mature. It enabled me to see the central role my mom (and other people) played in my life. It gave me perspective.

Since that moment thirty years ago, my relationship with my mom has only gotten better, stronger, and deeper.

It started with that list of love.

QR Code

See the Love List I made for my mom way back in 1988.

simplycelebrate.net/love-list-for-my-mom

"Thank Goodness We Did Not Wait"

I want to tell you another Love List story. For this one, fast-forward twenty-six years after the momentous day when I mailed that first Love List to my mom. At this point, I'm running my business—Simply Celebrate—a company dedicated to helping people love better, express gratitude, and celebrate the gift of life.

A woman named Sara subscribed to my Simply Celebrate newsletter, where she read about the idea of creating a Love List. She loved the concept and decided to try it out. In April, 2014, on her husband Chris's forty-sixth birthday, Sara and her three children surprised Chris with a collection of Love Lists.

Sara sent me an email to share how it went. She wrote:

"The kids and I made him a small booklet with our 'Top Tens.' He loved it! He never wanted us to go out of our way to buy him things, so it was just the perfect gift. He cried as he read them. Chris was like that, he would cry at just about anything that touched his heart."

I was so touched to receive that note from Sara. I could just picture the sweet, tender scene that she described—and I was thrilled to hear that she had taken the time to celebrate her husband's birthday with a Love List.

About six months later, I got another email from Sara.

She told me that Chris had been helping the children set up lights and audio for a Halloween party. He went to sleep that night and then awoke in the middle of the night trembling and unable to catch his breath. Sara asked if he was okay, but he wasn't even able to respond. She told me:

"He whipped his legs over the side of the bed, braced himself, and collapsed. He died instantly."

Sara continued:

"We would never have imagined that his forty-sixth would be his last birthday. I am so relieved and grateful that we created those Love Lists for Chris on his last birthday to show him how much we loved and appreciated him. Because he died at such a young age, we thought we had many more birthdays to celebrate him. Thank goodness we did not wait and that we made them that year. At his celebration of life, we framed our Love Lists and set them out on the table for everyone to read why his wife and children loved him."

I was so saddened to hear about Chris' death. Sara's words kept echoing in my mind:

"Thank goodness we did not wait."

What happened for Sara and her family is a powerful reminder—a reminder of why it's so important to express your love now, today, as soon as possible, rather than waiting until someday later. Do it now. Say it now. Life is so unpredictable—so if someone is precious to you, open your heart and let them know.

I've received so many stories from people like Sara over the years—stories about the power of sharing a Love List, about how this kind of gift can heal fractured relationships, strengthen a bond that's already wonderful, or open up new avenues of intimacy between people. I've heard stories about Love Lists being given at the breakfast table, during chemotherapy, at picnics, around fires, on birthdays, and at deathbeds. But you don't need to wait for a big milestone to create this kind of gift. Today is a beautiful day for a Love List. So is tomorrow. And every day after that. For as long as you've got.

Who needs a boost of love from you right now? What relationship needs to be healed, soothed, or celebrated? Who will you make a Love List for first?

QR Code

See the beautiful Love Lists that Sara and her children made for her husband's last birthday.

simplycelebrate.net/his-last-birthday-gift

QR Code

Watch a video conversation about someone who created a Love List for her parents and shared it aloud, just days before her mother entered hospice. **simplycelebrate.net/verbal-love-list**

QR Code

Listen to an audio workshop where I guide you through the process of making a really creative Love List, step by step. **simplycelebrate.net/audio-workshop-for-creative-love-lists**

More Ideas for Making a Really Creative Love List

Step 1. Close your eyes and imagine the person you love.

Think about the person you're creating a Love List for. It might help to close your eyes and imagine that person. Think about their beautiful face, or imagine sitting next to them in one of your favorite places. Let images come to mind about who this person is and times you've been with them.

Step 2. Set a timer and write from the heart.

Set a timer for ten minutes and let yourself write down anything that comes to mind about this person. Don't censor anything. Just write. Try to keep your pen moving and see what comes out.

- "I love your beautiful curly hair."
- "I love the little snorty sound you make when you laugh."
- "You are so generous with your kids."
- "You never miss your morning run."
- "You volunteer for the Special Olympics, and you inspire me to contribute more to my community, too."

I strongly recommend setting a timer so that there's a set amount of time for you to start this process. Otherwise, it may start to feel overwhelming or your Squawky Polly brain might tell you, "This is too much; we'll do it later." Setting a timer for ten minutes can help this feel a lot more fun and doable.

After ten minutes, you might feel like your Love List is done! Hooray! That's great! Or, you might want to keep working on it. If so, move along to step 3:

Step 3. Get inspired by photos and write more (if you want to add to your list).

Gather together some photos of the person you love: photos of them alone; photos of you together; photos of them with their colleagues, family, or kids.

You can look on Facebook or Instagram, on your phone, or in a photo album, or wherever else you've got photos of this person. Set a timer once again, and spend another ten minutes looking through photos and writing down anything that comes to mind. Some of these photos might spark new ideas for you—more things you want to add to the Love List!

- "I love that trip we took to Apple Castle when we ate caramel apples and couldn't get our teeth unstuck for hours!"
- "I love the blue sparkly shoes you insisted on wearing every day in Paris. (And how strangers would stop us on the street to admire them, and how we made new friends thanks to your shoes!)"
- "I love that every Thanksgiving we take the same photo of you holding the turkey platter, wearing your only-on-Thanksgiving frilly apron."
- "I love that photo we took in the Adirondacks when it was so blizzardly that you can only see your yellow hat and my pink hat!"

After the timer goes off, maybe at this point, your Love List feels done. Wonderful!

Or maybe you need to wrap things up here because you're pressed for time and the party starts in an hour!

But if you've got a bit more time, I'd encourage you to keep working on your list. In the coming hours and days, more items for your Love List will probably drop into your mind. At random moments—like when you're in the shower or stuck in traffic—your brain will go, "Ping! Another one!" and you'll think of even more things to add to your list.

Keep your Love List on your bedside table, or stored on your phone, tablet, or computer, just in case any more love-lightning-bolts pop into your mind.

Step 4. Add the finishing touches.

Whenever you feel like your Love List is complete, you can add a few special touches (like photos, doodles, or stickers) and choose how you want to present it. (See page 52 for some fun presentation ideas.)

But if you're really pressed for time, feel free to skip this part. Handing someone a handwritten list (with no packaging) is still wonderful! Even if you wrote your list on a Post-it Note or a restaurant napkin, it will still brighten your recipient's day. Fancy presentation is not required.

Step 5. Celebrate your efforts!

Don't skip this step! Really. I mean it. Take a few moments to appreciate yourself for being the type of person who takes the time to make a Love List. Acknowledge that you were willing to step outside the box, get creative, be vulnerable, and live your love out loud. This is a huge thing to celebrate.

Do not, I repeat, do not take this for granted about yourself. Take in a big, deep breath of appreciation for yourself, have a cupcake, listen to your favorite song, give yourself a hug—whatever you'd like to do to commemorate this moment. You just completed an amazing project that will make such a difference in your recipient's life—and in yours, too! This is definitely cause for celebration.

Still Not Sure What to Write for Your Love List? Twenty More Ideas for You

Sometimes, even when you love someone very, very much, your brain just draws a total blank and you can't think of what to say!

If that's happening for you, here are some ideas to get your wheels turning.

As you're making your list, you could share...

- A particular habit this person has. For instance, "I love the way you linger to touch plants when you walk by them."
- How this person cares for others. For instance, "I love the way you always offer to rub my head when I have a headache."
- Something quirky they do that you find so appealing. For instance, "I love the way you spread your cream cheese, so it covers every inch of the bagel."
- A funny inside joke that you share. For instance, "I love that we send one another Smurf-a-grams!"
- Things they bake or cook. For instance, "I love your banana bread. (Yum!)"
- Funny things they say. For instance, "I love when you greet me by saying YOLO!"
- Things you love that they don't do. For instance, "I love that you don't snore!"
- Things you love about their spirit. For instance, "I love how resilient you are!"
- Some physical attribute you love. For instance, "I love your Romanesque nose."
- Gifts they've given you. For instance, "I love the skunk baseball cap you gave me after we got sprayed during the baseball game in Anderson."
- Tiny things that sometimes get taken for granted. For instance, "I love the way you always recognize the holidays by sending me

greeting cards via snail mail. (And the five dollars you include, which I always use for ice cream!)"

- Funny things they love. For instance, "I love that you really, really love pickles."

- Some aspect of how they are with other people. For instance, "I love the way you and your teenage son play-wrestle in order for you to get a hug."

- A happy memory that you shared together. For instance, "I love that when we went to Hotel del Sol and I forgot my bathing suit, you suggested we buy cheap pajamas at Walgreens and cut 'em off at the knees."

- Something you always do together. For instance, "I love that you are my thrifting and hot chocolate buddy!"

- Specific things they wear. For instance, "I love your red sneakers! And that you pair 'em with purple laces!"

- Something funny or interesting that you noticed in a photograph. For instance, "I love the way you looked with all that Dippity-Do in your hair when we were bridesmaids at Susan's wedding!"

- Something about how you met. For instance, "I love that you're the kind of person who goes to libraries, since we never would have met if it weren't for the Bernal Heights Branch!"

- If you're making a Love List for your child, mention something you loved about them as a very young child. For instance, "I love the way you said flutterby instead of butterfly all the way until you turned four."

QR Code

See one woman's list of eighty reasons why she loves her mom—and a variety of other Love Lists people have written and shared.

simplycelebrate.net/eighty-reasons

More Ideas for Presenting Your Love List

Let's say you've written a list of ten, twenty, or a hundred things. Now what? You could stop right there and you'd have an amazing gift. As I mentioned earlier, even if you hand someone a plain white piece of paper with your Love List scrawled in messy pencil, it's likely to be one of the best gifts that person ever received.

But if you've got a little extra time and want to make your Love List extra special, here are a few presentation ideas:

- Write (or type) your list onto a colorful template. For a professionally designed template that you can print at home, scan the QR code on page 54.

- Add photos or artwork. Consider adding a couple favorite photos of yourself and the recipient alongside your list. Or add some silly doodles, cartoons, watercolor, anything you want.

- Roll it up. Roll your list into a scroll and finish it off with a pretty ribbon.

- Frame it. If your list is just one page long, you could frame it—just like it's a photograph or a painting.

- Make a Love List book. Buy a beautiful blank book and write one Love List item on each page of the book.
- Read your Love List out loud. Can you imagine sitting in a quiet place and reading your list to the person for whom you created it? This takes a little extra bravery, but it sure adds an intimate, loving touch.
- Create an audio or video recording. Read your Love List to your recipient aloud and record the audio or video using your smartphone.
- Make a Love List Joy Jar with fairy lights. If you have a couple hours—and about ten dollars—you can create a Love List that will really light up their life! You can find step-by-step instructions for making these on page 55 of this book.
- Create Love List Fortune Cookies. You can slip your individual "loves" into fortune cookies, giving your recipient the joy of cracking 'em open to discover all the things you love about them. Find out how to do this on page 60.
- Create Love List Easter Eggs, Advent Calendars, Valentine's boxes, and more. Check out page 62-65 to learn about these ideas.

One Million Love Lists...Add Yours!

Remember that Love List I made for my mom? I've made many, many more Love Lists since then—too many to count—and I've loved creating each and every one.

And today, I'm on a mission that I call One Million Love Lists. I want to inspire people all around the world to create heartfelt lists, totaling one million—or more. I hope yours will be one of them.

P.S. Keep a Copy of Your List

On my mom's eightieth birthday, I sent her the original list of one hundred things I'd written on her fiftieth. It was such a great gift all over again. We both enjoyed rereading that list. I encourage you to keep a copy of the Love Lists that you make, because you will enjoy them over and over.

Once you make your first Love List, you'll get to experience—firsthand—just how beautiful this project can be. Whether your list includes three items or thirty, one hundred, or more, this is such a powerful way to feel more connected to yourself and other people. It is truly the definition of loving out loud.

QR Code

Download the Love List Toolkit which includes two free templates that you can print out, fill out, and give out. This is a simple way to make your Love List a little more "fancy."

simplycelebrate.net/download-the-toolkit

QR Code

Let me know you created a Love List so I can count it toward the tally of one million lists. (We're getting closer every day—one list at a time!) It's easy to participate!

simplycelebrate.net/love-list-million

Sherry Richert Belul

I Love You #2

THE JOY JAR

55

The very first gift in this book was the Love List. Hands down, it's the best gift ever. Who doesn't want to hear all that love and admiration, right?

And as I said, you could scribble your Love List on a restaurant napkin and it would have a huge, loving impact. But if you have an extra hour or so—and about ten dollars—you can create an extra-special version of the Love List that I call...the Joy Jar.

Tucking all of your love inside a pretty jar adds even more celebratory oomph to your gift.

In the photos, you can see how magical the Joy Jar looks. You can tuck LED fairy lights inside, and your recipient will see sparkles of light and mysterious slips of paper. It's like a treasure chest!

Here's What You Need to Make This Gift

- A glass jar, fun canister, decorative box, or any other lovely container. (About four dollars at Target, Walmart, or Big Lots.)
- A string of LED fairy lights. (About three dollars a string on Amazon. Make sure to get the battery-operated lights that don't need to be plugged into the wall.)
- Some embellishments, if you wish: ribbon, buttons, costume jewels, small tchotchkes, crystals, meaningful tiny things that your recipient will love.
- Paper and pens to write your Love List. (Or a printer, if you prefer to type your list and print it out.)

Once you've got all your materials, the rest is super simple! Write your Love List. Then cut each Love List item into a little slip of paper. Tuck those slips into the jar along with your fairy lights and other embellishments. That's all! Done! You could also roll each Love List item into a little scroll, if you wish.

QR Code

Want to see a demonstration? You can
watch a five-minute video where I guide
you through the process of making your
Joy Jar with fairy lights.
simplycelebrate.net/love-list-joy-jar

A Few More Variations

If you'd like to put a special twist on your Joy Jar, here are
some suggestions...

- Fill the jar with favorite memories of times you've shared together.
- Fill the jar with things that make both of you laugh.
- Fill the jar with things you've learned from this special person.
- Fill the jar with things you want to experience with this person.
- Fill the jar with inspirational quotes.
- Fill the jar with your favorite inside jokes.

Try this for a group gift:

Email or text ten to twenty of the gift recipient's favorite friends
and family. Ask each person to send you three reasons why they love
this person. Print each reason on a separate piece of paper to fill up
the Joy Jar—and now, it's a gift from everyone! You can choose to
use people's names on their Love List slips—or not. If you make it
anonymous, then the recipient can try and guess who said what!
(When I've done this, people can always guess which slips are from
my teenage son!)

Try this for your spouse:

Every evening for the next month, write down one special memory that you shared that day.

- "You made me laugh so hard today when you sang 'The Star-Spangled Banner' in a falsetto voice when we were watching the 49ers game."
- "You surprised me by bringing home Pad Thai and a bottle of our favorite chardonnay."
- "Mmmm. Your good-morning kiss!"

Or, for your kids:

- "You started reading your first chapter book. I'm so proud of you!"
- "You helped Mommy make pizza, and then Toto ate the pepperoni we dropped on the floor."
- "You aced your chemistry final!"

Collect memories for thirty days in a row and then tuck them inside a special jar. Now it's a Joyful Memory Jar.

There are so many different variations on the Joy Jar. The possibilities are limitless!

QR Code

Check out a collection of Joy Jars—and get ideas for all the different variations that you can do! Scroll down the page, past the how-to video!

simplycelebrate.net/love-list-joy-jar

I Love You #3

FORTUNE COOKIES FILLED WITH LOVE

One of the best parts about creating a Love List—or any type of meaningful gift—is that your actions tend to inspire other people to create special gifts, too. You create a big chain reaction of love! Often, people take your sweet gestures and boomerang them right back to you.

That's what happened for me not too long ago. My beau, Ian, took my Love List idea and made it even better by incorporating a sweet, crunchy twist! He invented Love List Fortune Cookies!

Here's how it happened. One day, he showed up to visit and handed me a pretty box tied with a bow. When I opened it up, it was filled with fortune cookies. Whaaat? I couldn't figure out why he was giving me all of these cookies!

He said, "Crack one open!" When I did, instead of finding a preprinted Chinese fortune with some lottery numbers on the back, I discovered a slip of paper that said, "I love when we fall asleep holding hands." I opened another one, and in his tiny handwriting, it said, "I love the happy glee on your face when I carry our bags and your hands are free!"

Ian had created two dozen personalized "fortunes" just for me, and he'd magically gotten them into those little tiny cookies. I was enchanted. And of course, I insisted that he teach me how to make them, too!

He's generously shared with me—and now YOU!—how to create these oh-so-unique vehicles for your Love List. They are much easier to make than it seems. All you need to do is buy a bag of pre-made fortune cookies (which you can get on Amazon for about ten dollars for one hundred of them). Then you steam them open to exchange the commercial slips for your Love List slips.

QR Code

See detailed instructions on how to make these special Fortune Cookies.
simplycelebrate.net/love-list-fortune-cookies

I Love You #4

EASTER EGGS FILLED WITH LOVE

As you might be guessing by now, there are countless ways to present a Love List! Aside from a handwritten letter, scroll, book, Joy Jar, or fortune cookies, you can create special presentations for any holiday or occasion.

Here's a great one that will make your Easter baskets even sweeter...

Get a piece of paper and a pen. Make a Love List—a list of reasons why you love someone. (See page 39 of this book for instructions if you skipped that section.) Cut your list into strips, writing one "reason why I love you" per slip of paper. Then in your child's (or child-at-heart's) Easter basket, put one Love List slip inside each plastic egg along with a chocolate kiss.

You could also use a recycled egg carton. First, empty the carton so there aren't any actual eggs inside. Now, curl up your Love List items into each egg space, then add a few chocolate eggs if you want, close the carton, and wrap it with a bow!

I Love You #5

A VERY SPECIAL ADVENT CALENDAR

An Advent Calendar is a popular gift during the winter holiday season. You've probably seen one before. It looks similar to a regular calendar—except underneath each date, there's a little pocket that's filled with a small piece of chocolate, a piece of candy, or a toy. Every day of the month, you crack open a new date and find your prize inside. Sometimes it's hard to wait and you want to crack open the entire month all at once! But it's fun to be patient and open just one at a time, because you're stretching out the fun all month long.

To make a Love List Advent Calendar, first, purchase an Advent Calendar on Amazon.com or a stationery or craft store—or make your own. If you visit Pinterest and search "Advent Calendars," you'll find loads of suggestions.

Then, get a piece of paper and a pen. Make a Love List—a list of reasons why you love someone. (See page 39 of this book for instructions if you skipped that section.) Cut your list into strips, writing one "reason why I love you" per slip of paper.

Then, in each of the Advent Calendar pockets, put a Love List slip instead of (or along with) a small toy or candy. Now it's a calendar full of love!

I Love You #6

VALENTINE'S OR ANNIVERSARY BOX

Get a traditional heart-shaped box filled with chocolates—you know, the kind they always sell around Valentine's Day at practically every grocery store? Remove a few of the chocolates and discard them—and by "discard," I mean "put them directly into your mouth" and enjoy them! Ha ha. Obviously.

Get a piece of paper and a pen. Make a Love List—a list of reasons why you love someone. (See page 39 of this book for instructions if you skipped that section.) Cut your list into strips, writing one "reason why I love you" per slip of paper.

Then, in each of the empty pockets where those missing chocolates used to be, curl up a Love List slip. When the box is opened, your recipient gets an assortment of chocolate sweets and love treats!

This is a great gift for Valentine's Day, of course. It's also a great gift for an anniversary—the anniversary of your first date, first kiss, first time you each said "I love you," or something more traditional, like a wedding anniversary. Each Love List slip can be a "reason why I love you" or a "reason why we're such a great couple."

I Love You #7

BOUQUET OF FLOWERS WITH A LITTLE EXTRA

Buy a dozen roses or other long-stemmed flowers; real flowers, silk flowers, origami flowers, chocolate flowers—whatever kind you want.

Get a piece of paper and a pen. Make a Love List—a list of reasons why you love someone. (See page 39 of this book for instructions if you skipped that section.) Cut your list into strips, writing one "reason why I love you" per slip of paper.

Tie one Love List slip onto each flower stem by punching a hole in the corner of the slip, inserting a small length of ribbon, and tying it around the flower stem. Now it's a bouquet...with a surprise! This is such a lovely gift for Mother's Day, an anniversary, or just because it's Wednesday and you feel inspired to express what's in your heart.

I Love You #8

GRADUATION MOBILE OR A BULLETIN BOARD FULL OF LOVE

You can turn a simple Love List into a hanging mobile so your graduating high schooler can take your love along to college.

Get a piece of paper and a pen. Make a Love List—a list of reasons why you love someone. (See page 39 of this book for instructions if you skipped that section.) Cut your list into strips, writing one "reason why I love you" per slip of paper.

Affix each Love List slip to a hanging decorative item that has significance for the graduate. It could have a sports theme, a dance theme, or a science theme—whatever is meaningful for the grad.

Search in Pinterest for "DIY mobile" and you'll see dozens of tutorials for different mobile styles.

If making a mobile sounds too complicated, here's a simpler option…

Get a basic cork bulletin board either from Target or from an office supply store like Staples; you can also order one on Amazon. Make a Love List for your graduating student. Instead of creating a mobile, just pin your Love List to the bulletin board along with some meaningful family photos, inside jokes, stickers, and anything more you want to add for a little extra flourish. Now your college-bound student has a Bulletin Board Full of Love that they can hang inside their dorm room. During stressful moments (like final exam week), they'll have a big visual reminder that they are loved and cherished.

I Love You #9

COLLEGE GRAD MONEY 'N' LOVE PACK

Almost every new graduate appreciates...cash! But sometimes, giving a monetary gift can feel a little cold and impersonal. Here's an easy way to make this gift much more personalized and thoughtful.

Get ten crisp bills from the bank. Depending on your connection to the graduate, you can do ones, fives, tens, or twenties!

Get a piece of paper and a pen. Make a Love List—a list of reasons why you love them. (See page 39 of this book for instructions if you skipped that section.) Cut your list into strips, writing one "reason why I love you" per slip of paper.

Place each bill in an envelope along with a Love List slip. Seal the envelope. Decorate the envelopes however you like, or leave 'em plain!

I Love You #10

GREETING CARD BONANZA

My mother turned eighty this year.

Due to a recent loss in the family, she asked the family not to gather right on her birthday, but to wait and celebrate a few months down the road in the summertime.

I understood my mother's wishes for a low-key birthday, but I also wanted to find a way to make her feel loved and appreciated.

I'd already given her many lists of reasons why I love her, videos of family members expressing their love, and books filled with favorite memories and stories about her. I wanted to celebrate her in a new way.

An idea dropped into my mind one day during meditation, as ideas often do! I was reminded of something I've seen a few times on Facebook: a Greeting Card Bonanza. What's that, you wonder? It's where people post a request to their friends asking them to please send a greeting card to help celebrate someone's birthday. The goal is for dozens of people to send cards to the birthday person so their mailbox is filled with colorful envelopes from folks all over the world wishing them joy and love—a.k.a. a Greeting Card Bonanza!

I'd never tried this before, and it seemed like the perfect idea! After all, my mom had already received so many gifts that expressed the love and admiration from her family. Why not give her oodles of love from kindhearted strangers?!

I've had a lot of personal experiences of how a singular moment of kindness shared between strangers can have a profound effect. Every year for my birthday, I write love letters to strangers. It has been a practice of mine for the past six years.

My mom is also well versed in offering kindness to strangers. She often writes letters during my Birthday Kindness Projects, she gives money and pizza to homeless men and women, and she always takes homemade muffins or cookies to give away at Bingo games. My mom has a big heart, and she connects with people wherever she goes, always offering a compliment, joke, or baked treat to uplift their day.

So when I thought about the idea of organizing a Greeting Card Bonanza for my mom, I just knew it would be perfect. It would help her feel connected to people all over the world, and it would also respect her privacy during a time of sadness and loss. Instead of a big flashy party, she could have a quieter birthday celebration at home. She could open the cards whenever it felt right and enjoy a little moment of joy.

Over the course of several weeks, my mom received more than one hundred and fifty cards of all varieties—some lovely store-bought cards, some hand-painted or illustrated cards, funny cards, photo cards, you name it. She got cards from all over the United States as well as from India, Lithuania, Switzerland, South America, Australia, and England.

One woman who lives on the island of Guernsey sent a postcard because she knew my mom is an avid reader and loves a book called *The Guernsey Literary and Potato Peel Pie Society*. A few people enclosed a five dollar bill because they knew my mom always sends a little "mad money" in her own greeting cards.

People did all kinds of wonderful things like donating to the homeless, buying strangers their morning coffee, or offering to help a neighbor mow the yard. Then they'd say in their card, "Your daughter Sherry told me how you're always helping strangers. I wanted to follow in your footsteps and do the same. You inspired me to give and share with love."

Here's what my mom had to say about this gift:

"As long as people are sending loving letters to strangers, there is hope for peace and unity in the world."

Mom, I couldn't agree more.

How to Give a Greeting Card Bonanza to Someone You Love

- If you are using Facebook to post your request, make sure the person who will be receiving the cards isn't a friend of yours on the platform. If they are, you will need to direct message anyone you want to ask so the surprise isn't spoiled!

- You can also make a list of people you want to ask to send cards. Try to find at least twenty friends who would do this so it feels like an abundance of cards. Of course, you can request more—the more the merrier, right? Email or call each of these people personally to ask them. Tell them whose birthday is coming up and why it would be so special for them to receive a card.

- Feel free to use my idea of asking people to offer an act of kindness on behalf of the person who is celebrating their birthday. Telling them about the kindness in the card adds another layer of joy.

- Remember that you don't necessarily have to wait until for a big milestone like a birthday to organize a Greeting Card Bonanza. You can do this any day! Or, you could give someone a Greeting Card Bonanza for a different reason—maybe because he's going through a tough divorce, or she's recovering from surgery, or someone is grieving a death in the family or just needs a little extra love for any reason at all.

- If you want to have strangers send cards to your birthday person and you don't happen to have a loving community at hand, consider asking the local kindergarten teacher if her students could make cards. Or you could ask your book club, work colleagues, yoga friends, or some other group of friends.

You could also call a local senior center and see if they'd want to do a card-making project. Use your imagination to find a group of willing strangers!

A Few Hints and Words of Caution

- Don't give away the person's age if you think they wouldn't want people to know.
- Don't post the birthday person's mailing address publicly—or yours either, for that matter. Instead, ask people to direct message or email you and share the mailing address privately.
- If you're inviting total strangers to write cards, be discerning and use common sense to protect yourself. If you happen to have a PO box or a private mail box (PMB), give out that address rather than your home address. Unfortunately, there are some troubled people out there on the Internet who might not have the best intentions. So don't give out your home address willy-nilly.
- It can help folks feel closer to your birthday recipient if you share some things about who they are and what makes them so lovable. I created a document all about my mom and linked to some silly dance-party videos we'd made together so people could feel like they knew her a bit. I think this helped people write more personal notes. (Lots of people told my mom they loved the videos or the photo of her riding on a carousel.)

One Last Thing to Consider

For the past six years, ever since I started writing letters to strangers, I've been fascinated by the idea of reaching out to people I don't know with kindness and the huge impact it has. I'm not talking about the impact for the recipient—I'm talking about how it makes *me* feel to give love to strangers. The sense of joy and connection is amazing. Your first impulse may be to orchestrate this Greeting Card Bonanza for someone you love. But just you wait and see. It is a gift for everyone who joins in, including you.

QR Code

Listen to an audio message from my mom sharing how it felt for her to receive her Greeting Card Bonanza.
simplycelebrate.net/greeting-card-bonanza-gift

I Love You #11

GIVE A TOAST

I know this sounds so simple, but when's the last time you raised your glass and said a few words to appreciate, acknowledge, or celebrate someone?

Sure, we all do this at big events like weddings, graduations, and milestone birthdays. But the simple act of toasting someone can be a gift anytime, anywhere.

Try it tonight!

When you're having dinner with your beloved, pause to raise a glass and verbally appreciate them for something. It could be something very simple like, "Honey, I raise my glass to you for your patience this morning when I was crabby. You are the best."

If you're having lunch with your mom, hold up your coffee cup and say, "Mom, I raise my glass to you for all these years of being the gosh darned best mom you could possibly be to me. I'm so blessed to have you in my life!"

When you're with your children on the beach, raise up your plastic tumbler and thank them for bringing so much joy to your life. "Kids, you make me laugh every single day, and I love you forever. Never forget that."

Heck, try it with a stranger, too! Next time you go out to dinner and the waitress takes great care of you, surprise her when she comes to bring the bill by having everyone at the table raise a glass to thank her. She will be stunned!

Giving a toast is free, it's quick, and it will mean a whole lot to the person on the other end of that raised glass!

If you want to go the extra mile with this one, next time you're going to visit someone you love, pack up a pretty package of champagne or sparkling juice, a few beautiful glasses, and some lovely linens. Break it all out when you get there and create a moment of pure appreciation and joy with your surprise toast. Their jaw will hit the floor. It'll be a moment they'll never forget.

I Love You #12

JOYFUL JURY DUTY AND OTHER MISERABLE MUSTS

Have you ever been called in for jury duty? Some people actually enjoy it. But most people don't. Typically, you have to sit inside an uninspiring courthouse holding room for hours upon end, just waiting for something to happen. It can be a serious bore. Plus, you might be feeling anxious, wondering, "If I get selected for this trial, how long will the trial go on? Days? Weeks? Months? What's going to happen with my job? My family? I'm busy and I have so many things to do..."

Waiting in line at the DMV? Also seriously boring. Waiting in line to get a passport or see a notary public to get an official document signed? Not especially fun. Waiting to see a divorce attorney? Ugh. Waiting in the doctor's office when you're not feeling well and you suspect there might be some very unpleasant news coming to you? That's tough. Scary, too.

For life's dreary, boring, stressful, or wretched moments, wouldn't it be amazing to have someone sitting right by your side—holding your hand, making you crack a smile, helping you feel a little less alone? Imagine how good it would feel to have someone nearby, comforting you and saying, "We're going to get through this together."

You can be that special person. If you know someone who has a big appointment coming up and they're dreading it, offer to accompany them and provide moral support.

Depending on what kind of appointment it is, you can bring along some treats—fun magazines, snacks, a handwritten Love List—some type of surprise that will bring a little more joy into a dreary situation.

Let's say your friend is going in for chemo. When you show up to drive her to the medical center, surprise her with a tote bag full of goodies to help her feel as comfortable as possible during the session—maybe a soft throw blanket, fuzzy slippers, a special pillow, and some inspiring things to read. Or you could fill the bag with something fun you two can do during the appointment: a travel Boggle game, comics, a book you can read aloud, or some word-find puzzles. For extra oomph, Google "Make your Own Word Search Puzzle" and create a customized search that includes a special message by including words like *you*, *best friend*, *extraordinary*, *big love*, *good health*, or whatever words and phrases might feel meaningful for your recipient.

Try to include something funny to make your recipient laugh. You know how you have that private joke about rubber chickens always making everything better? Slip some rubber chicken band-aids into the bag or a rubber chicken in a Santa suit.

Your friend who is dreading a day at jury duty might appreciate an old-fashioned picnic basket filled with a thermos of fresh coffee, some blueberry muffins, a Scrabble board, and a book of Sudoku puzzles you can do together.

A worrisome doctor's appointment day might call for a beautiful bouquet of tulips and a great audio book she can listen to during the procedure.

Keep your ears open for when someone you love has an appointment they dread—and create a source of sunshine. This is such a loving gesture, and it can create a moment they'll remember forever.

I Love You #13

LOVE NOTE TREASURE HUNT

Maggie and Lacy live in a beach town in Oregon and have been together for five years. For as long as I've known them, I have never heard either person say one word that is negative or mean-spirited about the other.

In fact, when Maggie talks about Lacy, she positively glows with joy—and vice versa! They can't help but grin. They use the word "love" repeatedly. And if they were cartoon characters, you'd see their hearts gleefully boing-boing-ing out of their chests.

Maggie and Lacy are one of my favorite couples in the world because they intentionally love each other and they make choices to express their love consistently and often—in unique and creative ways.

They practice putting love into action.

Here's an example of how they do this. I hope you will try this out for your own partner, spouse, or children!

How to Set Up a Love Note Treasure Hunt

Maggie is a renowned photographer, and she travels a lot for her work. Lacy is a successful entrepreneur and life coach who also travels a lot for business. Very early on in their relationship, the two of them began a tradition of leaving each other a handwritten card when one of them was heading out of town. Lacy might hide a card in Maggie's luggage or Maggie might leave a card propped up on the kitchen table for Lacy to find later.

"We created a foundation in our relationship that we would always give each other something to stay connected while we were apart," Maggie explained.

She continued, "Then one day I was writing a card saying, 'I'm going to miss you. I can't wait to see you in five days when I return,' and I thought maybe I should create more things to keep Lacy engaged and connected while I was gone. So on an impulse, at the end of that card, I wrote, 'Clue: this gift we have is a token of our trip to the coast. What is imperfect to some, is perfect to others.' I knew Lacy would know that I was referring to a souvenir vase that we had which was cracked, but which we still loved."

Maggie explained, "I wanted my first card to lead her to that vase. So I then wrote another card to put under that vase. I also thought to write on the first card, 'Don't read your second note until tomorrow!' "

Maggie had hit upon the beautiful and delightful idea to create a Love Note Treasure Hunt for Lacy!

She ended up writing five letters and leading Lacy to them with clues, scattered in various places around their home. Each note reminded Lacy not to read the next card until the next day. This became such a fun way to stay connected the whole time Maggie was away on business.

Lacy told me that she loved finding each card and savoring it, waiting to open it the next day. "I would pour myself a cup of coffee in the morning and open up my card from Maggie to read. When we're at home together, we start our days together, so this was a neat way to still start the day 'together' even though we were apart."

Lacy continued, "Maggie and I love to go on adventures together. This gift made me feel like she and I were on an adventure together! There is so much excitement that happens in a moment of anticipation, and Maggie gave me that gift of the feeling of being on a trip together and looking forward to the next adventure."

• • •

Lacy told me that she and Maggie are huge fans of the book *The Five Love Languages* by Gary Chapman. This is a great book for couples. It's a book that explains that there are primarily five ways that people want to receive love: words of affirmation (like cards, letters, speeches, or toasts), gifts (a special handmade shirt or a thoughtful book), quality time (hiking together, seeing a movie together, or holding hands and watching the sunset), acts of service (doing the laundry or dishes for your partner, doing something to make their day a little easier), and physical touch (snuggling, hugs, massages, kissing, sex).

Most people have one or two Love Languages that they especially want and need. You can go online and Google "Five Love Languages Quiz" and take a free quiz to find out your primary Love Language.

For example, maybe for you, it's all about words of affirmation. You love getting a thoughtful letter from your sweetheart more than almost anything in the universe! It makes you feel so loved! Maybe words matter to you, but you don't really care about acts of service that much. If your partner mows the lawn, cool, whatever, but it doesn't make you feel loved in the same way as a romantic letter or note on your pillow does.

But maybe for your partner, it's the reverse! Maybe your partner loves when you do acts of service, like making her favorite sandwich or tidying up the living room, and maybe your partner doesn't actually care about flowery, romantic words as much as you do.

It's interesting to find out your and your partner's primary Love Languages, because they might be different! Once you know your partner's Love Language, then you can express your love in their language—which makes it feel extra meaningful and thoughtful. Your partner feels like, "Wow, you really know me and get me."

Maggie knows quality time is one of Lacy's main Love Languages. The treasure hunt was a way for Maggie to give Lacy quality time together, even though they were separated geographically.

Brilliant, right? There are so many great elements to this gift!

Here are some things I especially love about Maggie and Lacy's Treasure Hunt gift:

- It begins with an intention to stay connected even when the couple is apart.

- Maggie's first card would have been an amazing and loving gesture all on its own. But she listened to her creativity and took action immediately when the idea presented itself to write more than one card. She could have shrugged it off as "too much trouble," but instead, she chose to devote more time to creating an even more loving gift.

- Maggie also utilized the idea that dropped in about asking Lacy to open only one card a day. Again, a great idea got even better. By spacing out the opening of the cards, it kept the two of them "together" on this adventure for the whole five days Maggie was gone.

- Lacy especially appreciated the "anticipation" aspect of the gift. This is a great reminder that looking forward to things is a big part of being a loving couple.

- Maggie and Lacy both made it a point to read the book *The Five Love Languages*. They pay attention and apply the principles of the book to bring more love into their relationship.

What do you think? Are you game to try this? Next time you go away, how about leaving a Love Note Treasure Hunt behind! You can create a treasure hunt for your partner, your kids, your roommate, your BFF who's house- and pet-sitting for you, or for whoever's staying at home while you're away.

QR Code

For oodles of extra inspiration, listen to this twenty-three-minute audio conversation I had with Lacy and Maggie about creating this gift. They go into a lot of detail about how they intentionally keep their love alive in so many ways. You'll love it!

simplycelebrate.net/love-note-treasure-hunt

I Love You #14

HOST A SOIREE FOR AN ARTIST, WRITER, OR MUSICIAN IN YOUR LIFE

Do you know someone who paints, draws, writes, sings, or performs instrumental music? For their next birthday—or any day at all—ask them, "Would you like me to host a gathering of people for you, to celebrate your latest project?" You could host a concert, gallery show, book signing, or reading.

Many artists and writers seldom get the chance to share their talents publicly, and they may relish this idea!

You can make this as simple or extravagant as you like. For instance, you can have a gathering at your own home and limit the

86

guest list to ten or twenty people. Borrow some folding chairs, set up a table of refreshments, and you're all set to go.

(The photo on the previous page is from a small gathering I hosted for my playwright friend Tom. We had an intimate evening that included yummy food, a bonfire, and tiki lights. Tom treated us to a reading of a draft of his new solo show.)

Or you can research spaces in your community where a larger crowd could attend. You'll want to consider the type of space required and how much flexibility there is to bring in outside decorations, audio/visual equipment, and refreshments. If you choose to host the party at an outdoor garden, be mindful of the time of year and make sure to have a backup plan in case of stormy weather.

This is probably not the kind of gift you can surprise someone with, but once you've got the artist's thumbs-up for the idea, there are plenty of things you can do to add unexpected loving touches that are sure to delight.

Here are some things to consider:

- Do you want to surprise your loved one by inviting your own community of friends and family in addition to the guest list they provide to you?
- Can you provide refreshments that mirror the artist's work? For instance, some bakeries will decorate cupcakes with musical notes, an artist's palette, or even miniature book covers with actual photos. (Simply search online for "custom cupcakes with ____" and you'll see a host of ideas you can take to your local baker.)

- Are you able to design signs that include a photo of your loved one and some kind of fancy event description, just as if this were an event at an actual bookstore, symphony, or gallery opening?
- Do you want to write a special introduction for your friend, something you could read to introduce them to the audience? You could mention a little about their career, their latest project, how long they've been working on it, and maybe two or three reasons why you love this person so much.
- Can you create postcards of the event to give as souvenirs?
- Do you know someone who would donate their time as the event photographer so you could create a photo album as an added gift? Or if the event is a musical one, can you have someone make a high quality recording?

Lastly, don't forget the little ones in your life! If you know a budding musician, writer, or performer, hosting an event in honor of their talents could be just the encouragement they need to keep pursuing their art.

I Love You #15

DAYDREAM VACATION

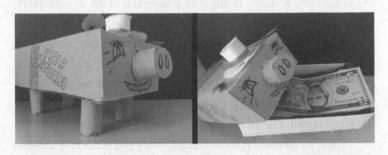

Do you know someone who's obsessed with New York City, Tokyo, Milan, or some other faraway place? Let's say she loves Paris—ooh-la-la!—but you don't have the time or Euros to take her there right now. You can let her know that you're paying attention to her dreams by gifting her with a fantasy getaway. I call this a Daydream Vacation.

For example, instead of booking two plane tickets to Paris, you could bring Paris right to your hometown. You could plan dinner at a fancy French restaurant or have croissants at a café (avec ambiance!) or try some French cooking right in your own kitchen. During your time together, play some French music, watch a movie like *Amélie*, or dance the cancan like you're at the Moulin Rouge. You could also spritz your recipient with French perfume and whisper, "je t'aime."

Try to create the experience that your recipient has been craving, even if you can't yet afford the whole enchilada (or coq au vin) just yet.

At the end of your evening or outing, give your lucky recipient a piggy bank with a little bit of cash inside. You can say, "This is a savings jar so we can start saving up for the real trip." Even ten or twenty dollars is a great start! Over the next few months, you can both add money to the Frenchie account. It might take several months or even years, but imagine the joy that you'll both feel when you count up the cash and realize, "We did it! We're going to Paaaaaarrriiiiisss!" Sometimes delayed gratification is so much sweeter than instant gratification.

My beau, Ian, inspired this gift idea. He even went one step further and made me a piggy bank, complete with a little gondolier's cap on the piggy's head. I loved the personal touch!

What's so spectacular about this gift is that you're not only showing your loved one that you want to help make their dreams come true, you are also giving them a taste of it now. Plus, you're creating the shared joy of anticipating the future trip together. You can start talking about the boat ride on the Seine, the art galleries you'll visit in NYC, or how it will feel to ride a horse across the wide-open plains of Montana, or wherever you're dreaming about going. You can plan together and enjoy the trip well in advance of packing and taking to the skies!

Side note: If you're in the San Francisco Bay Area and you know someone who's dreaming about a trip to Italy, you can take an authentic gondola ride on Oakland's Lake Merritt. I found this out—by total surprise—the evening when Ian took me for a motorcycle ride and drove to the lake, where a gleaming ornate gondola awaited us. The gondolier sang romantic Italian songs as we sipped the Italian wine Ian had thought to bring, along with beautiful glasses and some chocolate treats. It's not quite Italy, but it's definitely the next best thing!

I Love You #16

COMMISSION A WORK OF ART

If you're an artist, use your skills to show someone what a masterpiece they are! If you don't have a knack for art yourself, commission a piece of artwork in honor of someone you love. You don't necessarily need to spend tons of money to do this. There's probably a talented kid, teenager, or college student who would love the chance to create a cartoon, illustration, or small painting for thirty, forty, or fifty dollars—or whatever you can afford.

I have a friend who loves to illustrate people. She's always drawing people that she sees on the bus, at the library, or walking down the street. I commissioned an illustration of my mom, holding a pie and wearing her Conneaut Lake Park T-shirt. My mom loved it, and it makes me smile every time I see it.

Deanna helped her friend Nancy see her true colors by surprising her with a painting Deanna had done of her that was wildly colorful, radiating pure love. Deanna told her friend, "Nancy, thank you for inspiring me to find time to work on my art. I wanted you to see yourself how I see you—pure beauty and color!"

Commissioning a piece of artwork makes a beautiful memorial gift as well. It is a great way to pay tribute to someone's parent, grandparent, spouse, or child who has passed away. You can take a special family photo and invite an artist to recreate it, then get it framed, and it can be placed next to an urn filled with ashes, above the fireplace, or some other meaningful place.

When my niece's beloved cat Butter died, I commissioned a painting of Butter from my artist friend Greggie, who does amazing animal portraits. One of the things I love so much about my niece is her deep love for animals. I let her know that when I presented the gift to her. I wanted her to know that I saw her sorrow and that I understand and recognized that her deep grief came from her deep ability to love. And that is something I so appreciate about her.

There are so many possibilities. This is definitely a gift that allows you to go above and beyond, to express your love deeply, and to say, "You're so very dear to my heart. To me, you're a work of art."

I Love You #17

SEND AN AUDIO MESSAGE

A quick, easy, and very meaningful gift is to record a personalized audio message and send it via email. There's something extra wonderful about opening an email and being surprised to see an audio note inside. It's so unexpected! It feels secret and special. I think it harkens back to tape-recorded messages, like in *Mission: Impossible*!

You may be wondering, what makes this different than leaving a message for someone in their voice mail? Well, first of all, if you telephone them, they may pick up the phone. And sure, you could chat on the phone (that's always nice); but you might feel a bit tongue-tied, and you might not say exactly what you mean to say. If you record a message in advance, however, then you can really take your time, be intentional, and choose the right words to say. You can pause it, gather your thoughts, and then continue. Or you can delete the dang thing and start anew any time you want. There is a freedom in creating it and having the ability to restart if necessary! Plus, your recipient will be able to listen to your recorded audio message over and over again, as opposed to a phone conversation that happens just once!

That's my friend Susan in the photo on the previous page. She and I send each other loving audio messages all the time. I've saved all the ones she has sent me so I can listen over and over to her enthusiastic and joyful voice.

How Do You Record an Audio Message?

If you have a smartphone, it's likely that you already have an app called "Voice Memos" or "Voice Recorder." Most phones come with this app, and it makes it very simple to record a voice message. You can also use a free website like Vocaroo.com, which makes it so easy to record audio online. Just visit the site, hit the big red record button, and away you go! Hit stop when you're finished, and then you can email the audio to whomever you want. You can also download a copy of the file for yourself.

What Do You Say?!

Anything you want! Perhaps you want to appreciate your friend for a specific attribute she possesses or something she did. Your audio message could go something like this:

> Suzy, I want to tell you how much I love and appreciate the way you always reach out to people in need. I know that you organized all the dinners for the Martin Family after their dad passed away. You spent so much of your own time last week taking their children to the zoo and the park and helping the family survive the tragedy. But Suzy, it isn't just what you did, but also who you are. It is that you are the kind of person who cares so deeply. Your heart is so big and always open to everyone around you—friends, strangers, furry creatures. I want to read you a quote that always reminds me of you...and I hope you'll listen to this audio anytime you doubt how much you matter, because you make a huge difference in the world.

Perhaps your gift recipient lives far away. Perhaps they're working or studying overseas for a while. You could record an audio message to say, "I'm thinking about you and I miss you!" Or, if you're with a group of mutual friends or family members, you could do a group message and say, "We all miss you!"

For instance, I have a group of three close writer friends: Maya, Laurie, and Kirsten. Maya moved from California to New Jersey a few years back. Sometimes when Laurie, Kirsten, and I are together, we turn on the audio recorder and let Maya know that we are all together and we are missing her. We might tell her some snippets of stories. We might say what we miss about her. We'll describe what food we are eating, what we're writing about, what we imagine she is doing at that moment. Maya always loves receiving these group notes from her friends back home.

I like to end all of my audio notes with a poem that feels appropriate for the person on the other end. I think poetry can be like a mini-vacation for your mind. It gives the person a chance to close their eyes and let the words waft over them. Also, sometimes poets are able to more aptly say what I'm feeling, so I can borrow their words to express myself.

What Else Can You Record?

You can laugh, play the piano, share your favorite new song (or sing a song yourself), recite a passage from the book you're reading, have the dog bark hello, list ten reasons why your gift recipient is so awesome, describe what you're looking at right now (the view outside your window, your kitchen, a photo), invite the barista or waiter nearby to say hello, ask the stranger walking by to say a few words, record the street musician playing the accordion—anything you want!

Making an audio recording is quick and easy. Even if you record something very brief, just a three-second message to say "I miss you and I love you!" is such a delight to receive!

One Last Suggestion

I encourage you to create a folder on your computer where you keep copies of all of the audio notes you create. It's incredibly uplifting to listen to yourself talk about why you love someone or express appreciation. Also, you can regift the audio years down the road! Let's say you record an audio message for your friend on her thirtieth birthday. You could email that same message again on her fortieth birthday to re-appreciate her all over again—and give her a fun little trip down memory lane! I've done this with friends, and it is so wonderful for them to receive it again, especially if they've misplaced or forgotten about the original recording! What I usually do is send them a note that says, "I STILL love all of these things about you!"

I Love You #18

DESSERT OF THE MONTH

> This certificate offers the bearer exclusive
> membership in the
> Dessert o' the Month Club!
>
> Issued to _____
> First delivery on _____
> Baked with love by _____

People love to receive packages in the mail. And most people love dessert! (People who insist that they "don't like sweets" are very peculiar, in my opinion. But hey, to each his own!) And everyone glows when they know they are being thought about in a loving way. This gift combines all of those qualities: snail mail, sweets, and love!

There are lots of online shops where you can purchase a Gift of the Month subscription for cookies, cake pops, chocolate, wine—and that's great! However, you can also save money—and make the gift even more personalized and meaningful—by creating your own DIY version of this kind of gift.

All you need to do is make a homemade gift certificate that says something like: "Good for one sweet treat every month for a year."

QR Code

If you don't want to design your own certificate, no worries, I've created one that you're welcome to download and print right here.

simplycelebrate.net/dessert-of-the-month

And then pop your gift certificate into the mail! That's right. You will be mailing Aunt Emily a box of brownies, cookies, truffles, or biscotti every single month. Or if your recipient lives nearby, perhaps you can personally deliver the treats to their home, office, or school.

If you love to bake, this gift is perfect for you. But even if you're not a baker, don't worry. You can purchase the sweets, which can be lots of fun, too! It's especially fun if you purchase treats that feel extra meaningful to your recipient. For example, maybe they're obsessed with caramel, so maybe every month you purchase and send over a new type of caramel-related treat. Or maybe they love the color yellow, so you hunt for candy bars with yellow wrappers. You get the idea. Even if you're sending store-bought sweets, you can still make it feel personalized and meaningful.

While this is a sweet gift for anyone in your life, it is especially meaningful for elderly folks who are lonely or housebound. Those of us who have busy, full lives may not realize how life-changing it can be to receive something in the mail in the middle of a long, lonely day.

Some Tips and Extras

- Remember our Love List gifts from the beginning of this book? You could turn this Dessert of the Month gift into a Love List simply by including a "What's sweet about you" note in every box. For instance: "Aunt Emily: the sweet thing I'm appreciating about you this month is the memory I have of visiting you every summer when I was a child; you would make fresh lemonade, and we'd sit on your porch calling for 'Suzy' the blue bird and 'Sammy' the squirrel. I really thought they knew their names because you made it magical!" Or: "Aunt Emily, the sweet thing I'm loving about you this month is that you never forget anyone's birthday or wedding anniversary. You are so thoughtful."

- If you aren't a baker and you are buying your sweets for Aunt Emily, can you add a personal touch another way? Maybe add a handwritten card, draw a little doodle or cartoon, or print an old photo and write a memory on the back.

- If you happen to be the crafty type and you have some washi tape or stickers handy, decorate the outside of the box so it feels festive for Aunt Emily. (And for the postal worker!)

- This is a great last-minute gift, because all you need to do is send the gift certificate in the mail (print it, pop it into an envelope, done!), and that only takes a few minutes. And then you can send the first box of sweets a few weeks later, if you need a little time to get things sorted out. Your gift recipient will have the fun of anticipating a gift in the mail, coming soon!

I Love You #19

GIFT OF THE MONTH (WHATEVER YOU WANT!)

The previous gift item was a Dessert of the Month. But maybe your gift recipient is one of those odd people who doesn't enjoy eating dessert? Ha ha! Or perhaps they have dietary restrictions and they're cutting down their sugar intake. If that's the case, then you can choose a different type of monthly gift. Maybe a Bubble Bath of the Month gift, or Magazine of the Month, or Seashell of the Month, or anything you think they'd enjoy.

For instance, your literary friend would probably love a Book of the Month in the mail, hand-selected by you just for her! For another twist, you could give this gift a special theme—choose books by a specific author, books about art, books about the circus arts, gardening, baking, traveling, whatever your gift recipient loves most. The possibilities are endless! If you pause for a few moments, you can probably think of a theme that matches their passions.

You could include yourself in this gift by calling it the Book of the Month Club. Buy yourself a copy of the same book you send her—or borrow it from the library. Then, the two of you can talk about the book on your next phone call or coffee date.

Some Other Theme Ideas for the "Something of the Month" Gift

- Puzzle of the Month
- Comic Book of the Month
- Recipe (and Fixin's) of the Month
- Vintage T-Shirt of the Month
- Socks of the Month
- Hilarious Typo of the Month
- Postcard of the Month
- Coffee of the Month
- Tea of the Month
- Candle of the Month
- Lip Gloss of the Month
- Nail Polish of the Month
- Question of the Month
- Compliment of the Month
- Riddle of the Month
- Song of the Month (For this one, you could mail a postcard with the song title written on it—or, for a digital version, text or email a link to the song. Choose a song you think your recipient would love! Extra credit: say why you think he'll love this tune.)

I could go on and on...but you get the idea! This is such a fun gift, one that keeps on coming and coming and spreads cheer for an entire year!

I Love You #20

GIFT OF THE MONTH (*TRÈS PERSONNEL!*)

We've discussed how to create a Dessert of the Month gift—and how to put your own twist on things if your recipient doesn't enjoy dessert. Now, here's yet another twist—consider doing a monthly gift that involves one of your special talents. This makes it EVEN MORE personal and magical.

For instance, if you're a photographer and you know your friend loves wildflowers, could you send her a printed photo of some flowers every month along with a cheery note? Or perhaps you are great at illustrating, drawing, cartooning, or painting. Over the course of the year, you could send your lucky gift recipient a series of tiny works of art. Maybe each one could be of a different family member, or an assortment of trees, or her dog, Trolley, in a variety of playful poses.

See that photo on the previous page? That is a small piece of art my artist friend Greggie sent. It is my cat, Zoey. Truth be told, Greggie didn't send me an artwork of the month. But I can tell you, if he *had*, that would definitely be one of my all-time favorite gifts. As it is, this ornament ranks very high up on my list of favorite gifts!

Are you a singer/songwriter? You don't have to write an original song every month, but you might simply share songs you've written and send along some personal stories about each song, what inspired it, and where you wrote it.

Maybe you love writing; you could give a Memory of the Month by writing a short story or letter that illustrates a favorite memory you shared with this person. Add a special touch by including a photo each month that goes with your story.

Consider your talents—sewing, whittling, syrup-making, you name it—and package them up in a monthly gift. Ta-da!

I Love You #21

BRING A SINGLE FLOWER

On the way to my dentist's office in downtown San Francisco recently, I saw a flower stand, and, on a whim, I purchased a single orange Gerbera daisy for two dollars. It was cheerful and bright with a pretty yellow center.

When I got to the dentist and was led to the exam room, my dentist entered the room with her usual exuberant "Hello!" and we had a lovely conversation about our children, the theater, books, and clothing. (My dentist is a snazzy dresser, and we always like to exclaim "Oh my gosh, how cute!" over whatever outfit the other is wearing!)

Before she started examining my teeth, I told her that I used to hate going to the dentist, but that she is always so bubbly and positive that she makes it fun. I said, "I really appreciate that about you!" And I handed her the flower.

She beamed!

It was a small thing, right? Just one flower that cost two dollars. No big deal. But it was a bright gesture that meant a lot to my dentist. Think about it. When is the last time someone handed you a flower and appreciated you for something? It doesn't happen every day, does it? In fact, it is likely that it's been so rare that you can count on one hand how many times this has happened in your life!

I love gestures like this. It was simple and inexpensive, but it really made my dentist feel happy. And it made me happy. It was a moment that stood out in my day. And look, I'm still remembering it and feeling gleeful even now!

Giving a single flower is a great thing to do for anyone you know and like whom you want to appreciate. Consider the bus driver who always greets you with a hearty hello and who stops on a dime to pick someone up who has run to catch the bus but has missed the initial door closing. Think about the clerk at the dry cleaners whose hands are chapped and whose wizened face always breaks out in a grin when you walk in.

After some practice (because it can feel vulnerable), you may find yourself buying three or four flowers and giving a couple away to complete strangers, like the woman you pass on your way to work who always sweeps the sidewalk, the barista who always makes your coffee just right, or the girl sitting on the library steps reading Harry Potter.

You can simply hand someone the flower and say, "Have a great day." Or, if you're feeling brave, you can say why this person lights up your day, either aloud or in writing on a little card.

This can be a really lovely thing to do when you're celebrating a big moment or a transition in your own life. For instance, maybe you just found a new apartment or bought a house (hooray!) and you're moving to a new neighborhood way across town. You could hand out flowers to your local barista, yoga teacher, grocery store baggers, all the people from your old 'hood that you appreciate and whom you'll miss. You could say, "I've lived in this neighborhood for the last five years. I'm moving away soon, but before I go, I wanted to let you know that you've been such a bright, positive part of my daily routine for so long. Thank you. I'll miss you. I will come back and visit!"

For a little added sparkle, bring a short length of ribbon with you and tie a pretty bow around the stem of the flower. For double sparkle, write your appreciation on a tiny card, punch a little hole in the card, and then affix it to the ribbon. You're creating a big, heart-melting, jaw-dropping, WOW moment for your recipient—all for two to three dollars at the most.

I Love You #22

REMEMBER THEIR GRIEF

There's a phrase I often use: "celebrating in the dark." To me, what this means is being able to bring a little love, comfort, and light into a situation that's difficult, depressing, or heavy.

This gift falls into that "celebrating in the dark" category.

To create this kind of gift, first mark down the date when someone's beloved family member or friend passed away. Put a reminder on your calendar for one year later. Then, on the first anniversary of that death, send a letter filled with loving memories of the deceased—along with a beautiful card letting your friend know that you're thinking of them and you recognize their loss. Let them know you haven't forgotten.

Your letter might sound something like this:

> I want to acknowledge that it has been a year since your dad passed away. Suzy, I know how much you loved him and how you were his shining star. Please know that he will never be forgotten, even by people like me who only knew him through you. The stories I remember you telling me about him are so striking in that they reveal how much he loved you. For instance, I remember you telling me about the time your car broke down in Baltimore and he drove two hours in the snowstorm to come get you. I remember that you two stopped at a diner on the way back, and he bought you hot chocolate and shared his

own stories of car mishaps. I love thinking of that moment of connection and father-daughter love.

You might be thinking, "But is it really okay to send a letter like this? Maybe Suzy would rather forget about this sad event. Maybe it's not appropriate to dredge it up and remind her all over again…" In my experience, I've found that when someone precious has died, their loved ones don't want to forget. They want to remember. They want to honor that person and keep their memory alive. So if you write a letter (or record an audio message) to acknowledge the anniversary of someone's passing, 99 percent of the time, your recipient will be so appreciative that you remembered.

If you don't have a specific memory that you recall hearing, or if you never met the deceased, that's okay. Just write a couple simple lines that let your loved one know you are thinking of them one year later and you're sending your love. It can be that simple.

You can reach out on the first anniversary of the loss, the second, third, fourth, or every single year if you want. This is such a powerful way to express your love and let someone know, "You are in my thoughts."

Also, you don't necessarily have to wait an entire year before you reach out. Perhaps you know someone who recently lost a parent, spouse, child, friend, or even a beloved pet. There's usually a big flurry of love right when the tragic event happens: flowers, food, cards, and hugs. But what about five or six months later? Often, once the funeral service is over, most people get distracted and busy with their own lives, and they forget to keep checking in; your friend may feel very alone in her grief. You could put a series of reminder notes on your calendar to keep checking in with your friend once a month, just to say, "I'm thinking about you" and "I'm here." Your friend will feel so loved, seen, and understood.

A Few More Thoughts on What to Say

Many people feel tongue-tied in the wake of a tragedy. Often, we're not sure what's the "right" thing to say or do, and we worry about saying the "wrong" thing and making everything worse—so we hold back and wind up doing nothing at all. I urge you: don't do this. Even if you're not sure exactly what to say, just reach out and connect. If you need a little guidance on what to say, here is a general, all-purpose message that works in pretty much any grieving scenario. You can say to your loved one...

> I can't even imagine the type of grief you must be feeling right now. What has happened is just awful, and I wish I could take all of your pain away. I can't do that, but what I can do is say that I'm here for you. Whatever you need, you just text me, email me, or call me. If you want someone to just listen while you scream or cry, if you need a hug, if you want me to distract you for a little bit with a silly joke or just sit with you in silence, I am here for you. You are loved and you have a community to support you, including me. We are going to help you get through this. You're not alone.

Please feel free to copy and paste that exact message word for word and send it to someone you love who's going through a hard time. Or copy it but then add your own personal spin. Or record yourself saying those words, and then email the recording to your loved one. Choose any format you prefer, the key is just...reach out.

I Love You #23

LITERATURE LOVERS BIRTHDAY PARTY

When Susan's partner Jenny was about to turn fifty, Susan knew that a big bash was not a good idea.

Jenny is a self-declared introvert and doesn't like being the center of attention. A gigantic, noisy party with tons of fanfare? That would NOT be her idea of a good time. Months before her fiftieth, she started declaring to anyone who would listen that she was deathly afraid someone would plan a surprise party and that she would really truly not like it. (Hint, hint!)

Here's what Susan did instead...

Susan knew that one of Jenny's greatest joys in life is reading. Jenny has always been an avid reader, and she loves to discuss the books afterward.

Susan contacted a couple dozen of Jenny's best friends and arranged for each one to send their favorite book to her, each one a week apart.

Additionally, Susan nabbed Jenny's calendar and arranged for an hour-long phone call between each of these dear friends and Jenny. Since Susan knew that what Jenny loves best in the world is reading and discussing great books, this way she'd have months of doing what she loved best. (And she could do it from the quiet of her own home, wearing her PJs if she wanted—an introvert's dream come true!)

Susan's loving and thoughtful gift idea is a great example of truly listening to our loved ones and giving gifts that match who that person is and what they truly love—not what is conventional or what *we* want for them!

QR Code

Listen to my conversation with Susan about how she arranged this gift along with some helpful tips here.
simplycelebrate.net/literature-lovers-gift

I Love You #24

CELEBRATE A HALFWAY POINT

We live in a culture that seems to want to run us right past any accomplishments and on to the next thing. Go! Go! Go!

If we don't stop to acknowledge ourselves and whatever goal or milestone we've just reached, we simply keep running and are likely to get burned-out, stressed out, and bummed out.

Taking time to pause and pat ourselves on the back is so important; it gives us renewed energy and zest, and it lets us see how we've grown.

By the same token, it is important to celebrate along the way of whatever dream or goal we're working toward. If we are only focused on the end result, we might miss the joy that is on the path right where our feet are!

We've got to stop and do a happy dance on the journey!

Want to help someone you know do this?

You can!

Celebrate your friend's efforts when he is halfway done with a big project or has reached 50 percent of a goal. You can support him in keeping the momentum going with a gift of an inspiring book, an I'm-cheering-you-on card, or a humorous basket of half-and-half, half a cake, half cookies, a pint of Ben & Jerry's Half Baked ice cream, or half-baked bread (really, that's a thing; you can buy it at the grocery store).

Use your imagination to think up the perfect half-gift for your friend. Maybe it's a gift where you can deliver half now and the other half once the goal is complete.

Your friend will be so energized by your enthusiasm. It's sure to help him keep going, all the way to the finish line—and help him enjoy the ride!

I Love You #25

QUEEN OR KING FOR THE DAY

Do you know a kid (or a grown-up who's a kid at heart) who dreams of being a queen or king? Make them feel like royalty for a day!

Get her a crown and a wand, encourage her to wear her most glittery dress, and you can be her royal subject, planning fancy tea parties or extravagant outings. Let her decree what she'd like to do, where she'd like to go, and what she'd like to eat during the big day.

Consider a trip to the nail salon to treat her to a mani-pedi embellished with gems, glitter, or tiny fit-for-a-queen artwork.

Head to their favorite park or playground and stage a "royal photo shoot" so you can get some great photos of her that will make amazing gifts years later when she's forgotten all about this glorious day.

For added silliness, say, "Yes, your majesty," and be sure to curtsy all day long.

Sometime during the day, get down on one knee to present the Royal Declaration—a scroll you've made in advance that declares all of the reasons this queen (or king) is so beloved in all the land. (Not sure what to write on this scroll? Refer back to I Love You #1: The Love List!)

This is a fun, slightly ridiculous, and over-the-top gift. It's not for everyone—a shy, introverted person might not enjoy parading around with a crown!—but for certain people, this gift is just perfect! It will certainly be a day to remember!

I Love You #26

INTERVIEW KIDS OR ELDERLY PARENTS

This is another one of those amazing gifts that doesn't cost anything at all and takes barely any time, but it will be treasured forever. (I'm not exaggerating by saying forever! I mean it.)

The gift is an audio or video interview with someone's children or parents, asking them questions about their lives and about their relationship with the gift recipient.

Take a moment and think about the sound of someone's voice that you love. It is unique; it resonates with love and memories. It strikes a chord deep inside of you, doesn't it? (Hey, think about the word 'heartstrings'! Like musical notes.)

We love people's voices. But here's the thing, when someone is in our life for a long time, we likely take the sound of their voice for granted. It's something we hear all the time; it is part of the fabric of our lives.

But what we may not think about is that someday that voice will drastically change (as is the case with our children!) or will be gone forever.

Some of my most valued "possessions" are recordings of the voices of people I love.

When my son was four, his dad and I interviewed him on our audio recorder. You cannot imagine how precious that recording is now. He's almost eighteen now and has a deep manly voice, but when we made that recording, he still had his squeaky little boy voice. (Sigh.) I tear up every time I hear him talking about his favorite food (shushi!) and what street he lives on (California!).

When he was ten, I arranged for my son, his dad, and his dad's dad (Grandpa Bebop) to have a recording session at StoryCorps, which is a nonprofit dedicated to recording and preserving people's stories in order to build connection. (See my note below to find out more about StoryCorps!) In that recording, my son and his dad interview Grandpa Bebop about his life and people he loved. They ask about his childhood, hobbies, travels, and memories.

Grandpa Bebop died three years ago, and that recording has become one of our family treasures. Every time I listen to it, I feel as if he is sitting right next to me at the kitchen table, coffee mug in hand, spinning his stories and laughing that spontaneous hearty laugh of his! It's extra special because the three generations were all recorded together, sharing that moment in time.

I have so many stories of interview recordings! But let me share just one more with you. One Mother's Day, I read an article that my friend Roberta wrote about how difficult Mother's Day can be for single moms because there is no one to prompt their children to celebrate them on that day. It can be lonely.

That article gave me the idea to get her twelve-year-old son Ian on the phone and interview him about his mom. He was awesome. He answered questions about what he loves about her, his favorite travels with her, some daily rituals they have that he loves, and so on.

Roberta loved the gift at the time, of course. But here's what I know: she's going to love that gift even more in five, ten, twenty, or thirty years. Ian's voice hadn't yet changed. He hadn't yet entered those crazy teenage years. He was still a kid. The real gift to Roberta was capturing that moment in time and preserving the relationship between a mother and her little boy.

How and Where to Record an Interview

If you happen to have a StoryCorps booth near you, that is awesome. Using one is a wonderful experience that results in a professional recording. But if you don't have one near you or can't get an appointment, don't worry! All you need is a smartphone, really. You don't even need any special microphone or equipment. Don't let that stop you! I've done dozens of these kinds of recorded interviews (audio and video) on my iPhone, and the sound and video quality is great.

If you don't have a smartphone, you can record audio using a free website like Vocaroo.com. It's so simple. Get your computer. Open your Internet browser. Go to Vocaroo.com. Click the big red 'record'

button. Start talking. That's it! When you're finished, click 'stop,' and then you can save your audio right onto your computer desktop, or you can email it to someone or even share the audio link on Facebook or Twitter. It's pretty amazing, and it's so simple, anybody can do it with no techie skills needed!

Once you've figured out how you're going to record the audio, set up a time to meet with the interviewee(s), and make sure you keep it secret from the gift recipient. Ask some questions and voila...a very special gift!

Sample Questions You Can Ask Someone's Child

- What do you love best about your mom?
- Are there things your mom does to care for you or comfort you?
- Does she make you laugh? When?
- What are your favorite things to do with your mom?
- How does your mom make you feel loved?
- If your mom were an animal, what would she be?
- What do you think your mom loves best about *you*?

Sample Questions You Can Ask Someone's Parent

- What things do you love best about your son (or daughter)?
- What are some of your favorite memories of times you've spent with your son?
- What are you most proud of about your son?
- Do you have any traditions or rituals you do together?
- Do you remember any special stories from when he was a child?

- How about your own childhood? What are some of your favorite stories from when you were a child?
- What is the biggest life lesson you hope you've been able to pass on to your son?

If you can cajole the interviewee to sing a song, read a poem, play an instrument, or describe their favorite item, that will add some lovely texture to the interview. One time, my son's dad recorded my son Kayne singing a special happy birthday song that Kayne had written just for me. Right before I started writing this section of the book, I listened to that recording—he was twelve at the time—and my heart swelled.

QR Code

A few more sample interview questions.
simplycelebrate.net/
interview-questions

Editing, Formatting, and Presenting Your Interview

Once you've hit "stop" on your interview session, you can choose to simply upload that entire video or audio file to a flash drive (also called a USB drive or a thumb drive) and give it to your loved one just like that. You can also share the file using an online service like DropBox. com or GoogleDrive.

If you have a little experience with editing audio or video, you can add some special touches—fun music, photos, captions, your own

commentary, and so on. You can choose to highlight certain parts and cut others. If this is fun for you and you enjoy the creativity of it, go for it. But like I've mentioned before, this doesn't have to be a fancy or complicated process. If you feel overwhelmed by techie stuff, then skip it! Just whip out your phone, find your voice recording app, hit record, and it will be just fine and dandy! This gift can be very simple to create. It doesn't have to be an Oscar-winning production.

QR Code

Here's an example of a video that three teens made for their dad, in which they interviewed one another and then edited the footage in iMovie, which comes free on Apple computers. On this same page, you'll hear the audio interview I did for Roberta on that Mother's Day I mentioned earlier.

simplycelebrate.net/sample-video-audio-love-lists

And like I mentioned earlier, definitely check out the StoryCorps website (Storycorps.org) to find out more about this amazing organization. On the site, you can see if there is a recording studio near you, find sample questions to ask during an interview with a loved one, and listen to other people's recorded stories.

One Last Thing

If you are interviewing someone's young children as a surprise, let it be okay if they happen to spill the beans. "Aunt Ginny recorded me singing 'Twinkle Twinkle Little Star'! Did you hear it, Mom?!" For one thing, the child's mom may not totally understand what little Joey is talking about. For another thing, the heart of the gift is the recording and the moment in time you captured. If it turns out not to be a surprise, that's fine.

I Love You #27

INTERVIEW GUESTS AT A BIRTHDAY, WEDDING, OR ANY OTHER GATHERING!

We all know how milestone events can simply fly by. If you've had a wedding or birthday party yourself, think about how much you wish you could have cloned yourself so you could have had more time with every guest!

This gift helps the celebrant reconnect to that once-in-a-lifetime event and gives them a unique keepsake to remember it by.

All you have to do is use your smartphone to create a bunch of audio or video interviews that you can compile later in memory of this milestone occasion. You'll want to keep it simple, so before the event, think of one standard question to ask every guest.

For instance, for a wedding, you might ask, "What makes them such a great couple?" Or, "What is your best marriage advice?"

For a birthday, you could ask, "What do you love best about Ginny?" Or, "What makes Ginny unique in all the world?"

After the event, you can hire someone to compile all of the little video interviews into one movie. Check out Fiverr.com, which is a site where you can hire freelancers to do all kinds of small projects (including video/audio editing) starting at just five dollars per project. Or you can do it yourself using video editing software like iMovie, or audio editing software like GarageBand or Audacity.

My beau Ian and I gifted his brother and new bride with a collection of interviews of their wedding guests. Most people loved having the chance to give some sweet or funny advice and to wish the couple well. Ian and I had a blast doing the interviews. It was a great way for us to get to know the couple's community.

I also tried this out at my friend Laurie's fiftieth birthday party. Again, people relished having the chance to say what they love about her and to make some jokes or blow her some kisses.

QR Code

Check out these snippets of video interviews from a wedding and birthday! **simplycelebrate.net/sample-birthday-and-wedding-interviews**

Helpful Tips

- If you are doing interviews at a wedding, you should probably ask the couple about your gift idea in advance. Some people are very particular about every aspect of their wedding! If it is a birthday celebration—especially a surprise party—this can definitely be part of the surprise. If you're sneaky, the guest of honor may not have to know what you are up to and when you present the final gift, he'll be so amazed. It'll almost be like a second surprise party!

- Try to keep the interviews fairly short, especially if there are dozens of people at the event. Otherwise it will be tough to chat with everyone and it will be a bear for you to edit and compile later.

- It's helpful if you can get a guest list in advance so you have a checklist, particularly of VIPs—mother, sister, brother, BFF, childhood friend, and so on. Depending on the size of the event, it may not be possible to capture an interview of everyone, but do the best you can!

- If there are families at the event, consider interviewing them all together. The banter, interruptions, and little kids tugging at sleeves and giggling shyly can add to the fun!

- You can choose to simply wander around the event and do your interviews in a variety of locations. Or it may be easier to have a setup spot. For added flair, paint or draw some signs that you can hang near you! For Ian's brother's wedding, we set up an "Interview Station" in a small room near the ballroom where the reception was taking place. That way we could set up some good lighting, a place for people to sit, and a few fun signs. It was also a quieter space than the ballroom, so we could better capture the audio.

I Love You #28

LEAVE LOVE NOTES HIDDEN FOR SOMEONE TO DISCOVER LATER

Here's a little story from Roni, who is in my Present Perfect Facebook Group (facebook.com/groups/presentperfectgifts/), a place where a bunch of us gather to share ideas and inspirations about conscious and creative gift-giving. (By the way, it's free to join, and you're more than welcome to join the group!)

Roni posted:

> It may feel awkward to out of the blue just say "Hey, I love you," but it's important. Please do it now. I had a special relationship with my grandma. A thing I did for her once was to leave Post-it Notes hidden around her house that said, "I miss you," "You are loved," etc. I'm really glad I did that when I did, because I left her notes another time—one evening before I left her house—and sadly, she never saw any of them that time. She went to the hospital and never came home again.

Roni's story is the perfect example of how we just never know what today (or tomorrow) might bring. We don't know how long we will be here or how long our loved ones will be here. Roni told me that the first time she left those notes, it was accompanied by a terribly awkward moment. "I leapt out of my comfort zone, put my brave cape on, and asked my grandma, 'Would you want to be friends with me if we were not related?' I told her, 'I would still want to be friends because I like you that much.' She did not answer, just held my arm a moment and carried on making supper. But our relationship changed completely going forward. She became my best friend!"

I love that Roni was willing to leap out of her comfort zone in order to express her love to her grandma. I also love that Roni didn't wait. She could have put it off until it was too late. Instead, she got to have a best friend in her grandma!

Leave a quick love note for someone you care about.

As far as gifts go, this couldn't be simpler. Grab some Post-it Notes, small colored cards, or scraps of paper from the recycling bin. Jot down some short notes. "I love you!" "You make me happy." "You are awesome." For added oomph, you can decorate your notes or use printed notecards! Hide the notes in shoes, pockets, under their toothbrush, inside books—anywhere!

A Loving Twist

Create one appreciation slip for every member of your family. Use small cards and write, "I appreciate that you always tell us Spiderman stories at dinner to entertain us." "I appreciate that you never complain about washing the dishes." "I appreciate your quirky sense of humor and practical jokes." Slip these appreciations under people's drinking glasses or on top of their napkins at the dinner table. Have everyone go around in a circle and read their note before dinner begins. Feel the joy!

A Two-fer

My friend Myste got wind of this idea and decided to leave a love note for her five-year-old daughter on the fridge—every day—as a way to help her learn to read. Each note was one thing she loved about her daughter! Myste got to teach her daughter to read AND express her love all in one little note!

I Love You #29

RE-APPRECIATE A GIFT AND SAY THANK YOU ALL OVER AGAIN

Just the other day, I was wearing these really comfortable and pretty blue socks that my mom sent me about six months ago. (My mom has a philosophy that comfy socks are one of the paths to true happiness, so she is always sending everyone great new socks!)

I looked down at my feet and felt so happy in my pretty socks. Then I thought of my mom and felt so happy thinking about her because I love my mom so much.

On a whim, I pulled out my smartphone and pointed it down at my feet and snapped a photo. Next, on a better whim, I went and stood on the small woven multicolored rug she had sent me a few years back for my then brand-new work studio. Even though the colors have faded over time, I love that she sent it to celebrate my space.

Within a minute of thinking of it, I emailed that photo to my mom and told her I was wearing the socks she had sent me a long time ago and that they still make me happy. I thanked her for sending them, and for all the socks she sends me.

It took me less than a minute to snap the photo and say "thanks" to my mom. No big deal; it was such a small thing. And yet, when it comes to expressing your love...small things are a big deal. That photo strengthened the bond between me and my mom just a little bit more. It was an unexpected silly connection for us. It was an affirmation that the love she offers via socks is truly felt and appreciated—over and over and over, even on the many days I never think to mention it.

Here's another re-appreciation story: I have a friend whom I met at a camp for adults a few years ago. I joked with him that I wanted a cozy flannel shirt like his. He surprised me by buying me one and mailing it to me a few weeks after I got home from camp! That shirt is so cozy and feels like love, so I take it with me on my quarterly personal retreats at a little cabin on a hill. Each time I'm there, I remember to take a photo of myself in that flannel shirt so I can send it to him and thank him again. (That's me in the photo above, wearing the shirt Jeff gave me, with the cute little cabin behind me!)

Recently, I wrote to the college writing professor who encouraged me to participate in a New York City Arts Program for a semester. At that point in my life, I had never lived in a town larger than five thousand people. I felt drab and ordinary. I was so depressed by my plainness. I didn't think I belonged in a place like New York City. But this professor didn't see a plain girl—he saw great potential in me. He helped me get an internship at a big magazine—and so I lived in NYC for a semester, and it completely changed my life. This recent letter was the third or fourth letter I've written to that professor. His belief in me and what he saw in me shaped my entire life. I now live a wonderfully creative life in San Francisco, and I can't thank him enough. Literally! I'm sure that won't be the last time I thank him!

Look around your house. Are there some items you received as gifts years ago that you still cherish? How about wedding gifts, or maybe a photograph someone took of you that captured an important moment? Did a friend show up for you when you were grieving and you still remember the feeling of love? Let that person know you are still grateful! Say thank you all over again with a card, a text, a photo plus a text, any way you want. Re-appreciate the love you've received in the past—and send love right back.

I Love You #30

HOST A BUBBLE FLASH MOB

Do you have a friend who is really bubbly and amps up the room with her effervescence when she enters it? What if you gave her a gift that's an experience of what her friendship feels like to you? Host a Bubble Flash Mob in her honor!

What you want to do is arrange a time to hang out with your friend at a local park. Maybe tell her you want to have a picnic together or that you need some help plotting out your new novel. Find a reason to schedule a specific time—and make sure nothing happens to upend your schedule!

You can invite as many people as you want to help make up your "mob," but if you invite friends of the gift recipient, you'll want to make sure they are somehow in disguise or that they aren't visible to your friend from wherever you two are situated in the park. If you invite people your friend doesn't recognize, have them arrange themselves fairly close to your own picnic blanket in the park—casually collecting around you but not letting on that they know you.

You will have told everyone in advance to bring a jar or tub of bubbles. There are also awesome bubble blaster guns that easily shoot tons of bubbles. Also, you can purchase bubble wands and even great big bubble makers! (See note below about bubble possibilities!)

Important: Make sure no one shows any signs of having bubbles with them! If people are bringing children, you might advise them not to tell the kids in advance, because often kids will unintentionally blow the cover by blowing bubbles early! They can't help themselves; it is so much fun! (Also, if people don't tell their children, the bubbles will be a magical surprise for the kids, as well as for your friend!)

At the preset designated time, you will be ready to whip out your own bubble blaster and cue everyone that the flash mob is on. (You could also have another signal, like suddenly standing up and waving to someone in the crowd.)

When you give the "GO!" sign, everyone you've invited should stand up, circle around you and your friend and blow bubbles to their heart's content. Try to keep it going for at least a full minute or more!

Wowwwwwweeeee! Let the enchantment abound—and surround you!

Your friend will be awed and amazed. This would be a good time to whisper to her, "This is what your friendship feels like to me. You bring joy everywhere you go. You are magical!"

Now that the surprise has happened and the bubbles are floating all over, if you want, you can hand out small containers of bubble solution to everyone nearby in the park who may have gathered to happily gawk, especially to children, who will be enchanted and start to toddle toward your bubble mob! (Obviously, you need to think ahead to bring extra bubble solution and discreetly hide it in your bag! You can buy small bubble containers by the dozen at your local party store.)

A Few More Bubbly Ideas

- This is a wonderful gift for a child in your life! And it will be easier to pull off because they likely won't know a lot of the adults you invite. Or even if they do, they won't suspect anything unusual.
- Google "really big bubbles" or "giant bubbles" to learn how to easily make cow-size bubbles.
- Check party stores or online stores for oodles of bubble solutions, machines, and makers. There's no lack of bubble makers in this universe!
- Designate someone in advance to be your photographer, and make sure they take lots of photos that include you and the gift

recipient. Part of your gift can be a small photo album with a dozen of the best photos from the event. For added oomph, in that album include short stories of times you've spent with your friend that have felt bubblicious.

P.S. The photo at the top of this chapter was taken by my friend, Andrea Scher, who is a professional photographer and someone who loves to make magic happen!

QR Code

I've got more tips for you! Watch this delightful five-minute video that tells you everything you need to know about how to host your Bubble Flash Mob. Also: links to bubble resources to make your planning simpler!

simplycelebrate.net/bubble-flash-mob-how-to

I Love You #31

FAMILY RECIPE BOOK

This gift idea—creating a family recipe book—is far from quick and easy, but it's infused with such a yummy combination of heart, history, and practicality. It's a gift that will leave a major impact on your recipient, for sure! One of the best things about this gift is that once you create it, you'll not only have a gift that you can give to everyone in your clan right now, you can keep on gifting it to all the generations to come.

The first thing you want to do is to make a list and gather the recipes for all of the family faves that folks have been cooking for years. Yes, add Aunt Edna's "Cool Beans Crunch." Definitely don't forget the "Smith's Delish Dish" or "Rosa's Christmas Roast Beast." You could have a whole section on competing chocolate chip recipes if there's a little culinary sibling rivalry in the clan.

You can ask your family for their favorites to share and have them pass along the recipes to you. They might guess that you're cooking something up, but they won't know for sure. (And by the time you finish the book and gift it to them, they'll have long forgotten!)

To go above and beyond, write down any stories people tell you as they are passing along the recipes. When you are on the phone with your sister and she laughs about how every time your brother makes stew, he includes a "mystery" ingredient and everyone has to guess what it is—oh, and one time it was Pop Rocks—that's the kind of thing you want to remember for your book. It's really fun to include stories and quotes alongside the recipes.

Hunt down any family photos that might relate to cooking or baking. For instance, don't you have a photo of Grandma Eva rolling out the strudel dough at the huge dining room table back in the '80s? And isn't there a snapshot someplace of Uncle Tony grinning sheepishly as he showcases two teeny beets he grew in his backyard garden? Do you have any of those classic family shots of everyone seated at the dinner table where you can hardly see anyone's faces and the big salad bowl is blocking little Sarah almost completely, so all you see is her tiny hand raising a fork? Insert those kinds of photos to add even more charm and personality to your book.

Make sure that you're finding plenty of ways to appreciate each of the people whose recipes you're including. You can do this with a special Editor's Note at the beginning of each recipe; for instance, "Aunt Edna always looks fabulous in her red dresses while making those carrots!" Or, "Mama could always cook and carry on five conversations at once. I don't know how she did it!"

Once you've collected all of your recipes, stories, quotes, and photos, you can create the book in a variety of ways. Depending on your budget, this can be a complete do-it-yourself project. Or you can hire someone to help input, scan, and design it.

You can paste things on sheets of paper and scan those sheets so it has a scrapbook look, hopefully including people's actual handwritten recipes. Or you can format all the text in the same font so it has a more polished look. You can use a generic bookmaking service you find online by searching "online photo books" or "custom photo books online." There are even companies that are dedicated to creating family recipe books. You can find these by searching "custom recipe book" or "personalized family recipe book."

No matter how you create or present the book, I can assure you of this: when you give this gift, your family will most definitely think it is the greatest thing since sliced bread. You'll have them eating out of your hands!

I Love You #32

CELEBRATION BOOK (THE GIFT OF A LIFETIME)

In Celebration of Your Wedding
With All Our Love...

When my best friend Lisa was getting married many years ago, she said to me, "Don't buy us a gift; I want you to make us something." Lisa knew that I loved personal kinds of gifts, and I'm sure she wanted to encourage my creativity, but also wanted to help with my then very squeezed budget!

Holy Toledo! What could I make for her and David that would be special enough for their wedding? I was honestly really worried that I wouldn't be able to come up with something.

Well, I didn't. Life did!

Nothing came to me while I was thinking, thinking, thinking. But then I awoke in the middle of the night, and there was an idea, just gifted to me from wherever beautiful ideas originate!

Here's what I heard in my head: "Interview the bride, groom, and the wedding party and find out what makes this wedding so important. Get stories about the couple. Showcase the meaning behind the wedding—two people who love one another and a whole community that loves and supports them."

I drafted a letter to send to every bridesmaid, every groomsman, the parents of the couple, the couple's siblings, and their best friends. I told them I wanted to surprise Lisa and David with a book of love that would always remind them of what a great couple they are, what their marriage really means, and how much they are loved.

I asked people to respond to a few questions and to also send me a few snapshots of themselves with Lisa and David. (This was back before digital photography was common!)

I also wrote letters to Lisa and David telling them that I didn't want them to know what I was doing, but that I needed them to respond to some questions and send me some of their favorite photographs of themselves and with family and friends.

This project was so much fun for me. Every time I would get responses back, I would cry. They were so touching.

I scanned all of the photos, formatted the text, printed out the pages, and created a book for Lisa and David that included their own responses and photos, but also those of their closest friends and family.

When I presented the book to Lisa and David at the wedding celebration brunch, as soon as they opened it up and started reading, I knew it was the perfect gift. They passed it around, and people laughed and cried. Some folks read portions out loud. I looked around and saw how that book connected everyone in exactly the way I had hoped.

Lisa and David received a lot of wonderful gifts that afternoon—from flatware to ceiling fans—but this book was the gift that truly reflected to them the meaning behind all of us being gathered there.

It made their love tangible.

Fast-forward to twenty years later, and Lisa and David are still happily married. But of course, like all marriages, it has occasional bumpy moments. Lisa told me recently that sometimes when things are hard between her and David, she pulls out that wedding book and reads through it to remember the solid foundation of love that they share and all of the beautiful stories and people that make up their life.

You can create a book like this for a milestone occasion for someone you love: weddings, birthdays, anniversaries, retirement, or to commemorate the end of someone's life.

Steps to Creating a Celebration Book

Make a list of everyone closest to the book recipient(s) and find their email addresses or mailing addresses.

- Come up with four or five questions you want people to answer. You can invite them to simply write something, like a letter or a card, but in my experience, people tend to write generic platitudes or general "best wishes" kinds of things that don't really say much. That's why asking a few specific questions is often better.

- Contact each of these participants and invite them to respond to the questions by a certain timeline. Also ask them to send a few photographs and/or draw something for the book.

- Follow up with people a few times. Humans love to procrastinate. Gentle, loving reminders will go far!
- You can choose to scan, format, and design the book, or you can simply create a more scrapbook-style book by pasting text and photos into an album directly.

QR Code

I've created a step-by-step Celebration Bookmaking Course that includes checklists, email templates, resources, and inspirational videos to make it simple for you. I also have a done-for-you bookmaking service.

simplycelebrate.net/diy-celebration-book-class

I Love You #33

THE GREATEST GIFT OF ALL: A MOMENT OF YOUR UNDIVIDED ATTENTION

Oh! I can't believe we've already come to the end of this book. I loved sharing so many ideas with you. And I have so many more to share in the future!

Isn't it wonderful to create a special gift or experience for someone when you've thought ahead and added all kinds of lovely touches? I find great joy in the planning and giving of gifts. These celebrations saved my life, as you know. And every day they help me feel alive and connected. Making these kinds of intentional gifts is life-affirming and joy-inducing, for sure.

But you know what else is wonderful: to create one tiny, magical moment for someone by showing up with all the presence you can muster.

Before you pooh-pooh this idea and flip back through the book for something weightier and tangible, hold on and read the next few paragraphs!

Consider how many times a day you are with people and they are only half there with you. You can tell that they are thinking about the next thing they want to do or say. They might be glancing at their phone or even staring at a computer screen. There's a distance in their eyes and a lackluster tone to their voices.

They're kind of like automatons, right? Here, but not here.

We all long to feel seen, loved, and connected. Yet how often are most of us taking the time to consciously be here with the people in our lives?

As you go about your day today, I want you to think of your presence as a gift. Start with your children as you are hurriedly getting your things together to rush out to school and work. As they fly out the door, you might typically give them a distracted kiss on the top of their heads, sometimes missing the target altogether and kissing the air instead. Today, stop them gently with your hands and look them in the eyes. Tell a little inside joke, or use a phrase that always makes them laugh. Tell each one, "I love you." And pause. Don't rush past this moment with these people who mean more to you than you can ever describe.

At work, intentionally find something to compliment your coworkers on, one by one. No, don't be fake. I mean an authentic compliment. Tell Nancy you so appreciated all the time she put into that Danson Report. Tell Jane her new hairdo truly suits her and brings out her sass. Mention to John that you were inspired by the way he spoke up at the board meeting yesterday. Again, make that pause happen. Your gift, remember, is this tiny magical moment. What makes it magical is the presence you bring and the presence you invite them into.

Try it with strangers, too. On your way home from work, when you zip into the bakery to pick up some olive bread, look the baker in the eye and say something like, "I want you to know this bread always makes my daughter so happy. She designs faces on her plate with the olives and then gobbles them up. You're not just baking bread, you are adding to our family's happiness! Thank you."

Please don't disregard this last gift. I deliberately put this one at the end of the book to give it the most weight.

Most people wake up and go about their day as if it isn't a miracle. We forget that this adventure on planet Earth that we share with seven billion others is temporary. Every once in a while, when someone we love dies or when we're hit with a critical illness, the veil lifts and we remember how truly precious every single minute is.

Can we find a way to express that preciousness in our everyday life? Can we gift it to others?

Here's what I want to leave you with:

Our lives are made up of singular moments.

We have the choice to make our moments memorable.

And making magical moments can be the biggest gift to ourselves—and to others.

FINAL THOUGHTS

Never underestimate the power of a single expression of love.

Remember at the start of the book, when I told you my story about the pinpricks of light?

This is your chance to never forget that a single moment of your love and presence is a gift of light to everyone around you. Every gesture of love you make, every kindness, every heartfelt word of encouragement is a gift. *You* are a gift. (In fact, the light of your presence is the very best gift of all!)

We have the choice to create magical moments for ourselves and for the people around us. Knowing this and acting in service to it is our best chance to live the life we've always imagined—one that is full of sweetness, joy, and color.

Turn ordinary days into an extraordinary life, moment by moment by moment.

Try it and see. And let me know how it goes.

I love hearing stories of imaginative and impactful gifts! Will you write and tell me about a creative gift you've given or received? You can bet...your story will be a pinprick of light for me!

xo

Sherry

Sherry@simplycelebrate.net

QR Code

If you make a Love List for someone—or many someones!—as I hope you will, please take a moment to add each one to my Love List Counter. I'm on a mission to inspire one million Love Lists.

simplycelebrate.net/love-list-million

RESOURCES

Companies

Storycorps

storycorps.org • Storycorps' mission is to "preserve and share humanity's stories in order to build connections between people and create a more just and compassionate world." Check out their online resources for interviewing your family and friends, or make an appointment for an in-person interview in select cities.

Postagram

sincerely.com/postagram • Turn your photo memories into easy-to-send postcards with this simple app. All you do is upload your photo, type in your message to your loved one, add their address, and voila—instant love on a real postcard arriving in their mailbox in about a week.

Compendium Pop-Open Cards

www.live-inspired.com/ThoughtFulls-Pop-Open-Cards-C262 • These small pop-open cards each contain an uplifting or inspiring quote. They are perfect to enclose in any letter or greeting card. Or you can tuck one in your loved one's shoe, purse, or pocket! It's like receiving a tiny gift!

Etsy

www.etsy.com • Try searching in Etsy for custom bookmarks, custom aprons, custom tattoos, custom balloons, custom anything! If you have a creative spark and you need some assistance, you will likely find it on Etsy!

Fiverr

www.fiverr.com • Fiverr is a great place to go for help if you want to have someone create a piece of art or a customized graphic for a gift you are making. Scroll through their options, and it might spark an idea for a voiceover, video, Hollywood star, or crazy custom logo for someone you love!

Personalization Mall

www.personalizationmall.com • This website has tons of personalized gifts, but my favorite is to have them make photo ornaments. For just ten to twenty dollars, you can have an ornament made from a photo memory. These don't have to be only for Christmas trees; your friend or family can hang them anywhere, to enjoy anytime.

Vocaroo

vocaroo.com • This online voice recorder can be used instead of your phone's recorder if you want to easily send a loving audio note to someone in your life. It is simple and free to use!

Inspiring Books

The Power of Moments: Why Certain Experiences Have Extraordinary Impact • Chip Heath and Dan Heath

The Five Love Languages: Secrets to Love that Lasts • Gary Chapman

Giftology: The Art and Science of Using Gifts to Cut Through the Noise, Increase Referrals, and Strengthen Client Retention • John Ruhlin

50 Ways to Say You're Awesome • Alexandra Franzen

Big Magic: Creative Living Beyond Fear • Elizbeth Gilbert

What You Practice is What You Have • Cheri Huber

The Charge: Activating the 10 Human Drives that Make You Feel Alive • Brendon Burchard

Thank and Grow Rich • Pam Grout

Outrageous Openness • Tosha Silver

Essentialism: The Disciplined Pursuit of Less • Greg McKeown

Modern Loss: Candid Conversation about Grief.Beginners Welcome.• Rebecca Soffer and Gabrielle Birkner

Modern Love • Daniel Jones

QR Code

I will keep updating this list of resources for you to include even more support for your creative gift-giving endeavors. Check back again and again! **simplycelebrate.net/say-it-now-resource-list**

ABOUT THE AUTHOR

As the founder of Simply Celebrate, Sherry helps people celebrate who they are and the people they love through one-of-a-kind imaginative and impactful gifts, life coaching, and inspirational books and articles.

Sherry's mission is to inspire people of all ages to celebrate the gift of life—and to say "I love you" at every possible opportunity. Her motto is: "Say it now." Don't wait to express how you feel.

Sherry's creative gift ideas have been featured in *Town & Country*, *Brides*, *Modern Bride*, *InStyle*, *Redbook*, the *San Francisco Chronicle*, *Nickelodeon Parents Connect*, *Bay Area Parent*, the *Huffington Post*, and on a variety of podcasts and radio shows.

She lives in the Bay Area of California with her son, his dad, her partner Ian, and an ever-growing collection of fun, whimsical hats.

More info about Sherry's work can be found at simplycelebrate.net

GRATITUDE

So many people helped make this book possible! Oh my goodness—I could easily fill a two-hundred-page document with gratitude notes.

Here are just a few people who helped to birth this book—people who chimed in with helpful edits and feedback, people who sent words of encouragement to urge me to keep going, people with wonderful design and proofreading skills, and more:

Alexandra Franzen, who can make magic with her editing and copywriting skills. Alex is also a master of expressing love and appreciation, which makes her the perfect midwife for this book.

The team at Tiny Press and Mango Publishing who brought oodles of talent and heart to this project.

Tamara Monosoff who insisted I begin this book "right now" and who generously provided so much author training, including the idea for the QR codes in this book.

My writer friends: Susan Harrow, Maya Stein, Kirsten Soares, Laurie Wagner, Ellen Fondiler, Alison Luterman, Nan Seymour, and Chris Fraser, who inspire and support me every day in countless ways.

Patti Digh and the Life is A Verb Camp Community who offer courage, heart, and creativity on an ongoing basis.

Team BFF: Carrie Roldan, Rachel Archelaus, Jean Berry, Cindia Carrere, RoseAnn Janzen, and Dawn Andrews for their pegacorn magic and infinite support.

My clan, Kayne Belul, Bob Kayne, and Ian Fratar, who all bring such presence, joy, and humor to my life. They are my daily gifts. They are the family I always dreamed of.

Cheri Huber and the Zen Monastery Peace Center, which has provided a foundation of awareness, presence, and joy in my life since 1991.

Tricia Huebner, my dear friend and weekly mastermind partner whose wisdom and encouragement have cheered me on for thirty years.

Linda Murnane Ryan, who has also been a weekly mastermind partner, an avid fan of the Love List, and the most enthusiastic cheerleader ever!

Brendon Burchard, Denise Burchard, Momma B, Denise McIntyre, and the entire B Crew Team who teach me new ways to live better, love better, and "bring the joy" every single day.

The Simply Celebrate community, who continually seek the pinpricks of light and who share their gift ideas and love with me.

Everyone in this book who shared their beautiful stories with me and gave permission for me to use them: Andrea S, Cindia C, Deanna B, Elina T, Greggie B, Jeff H., Jenni R, Lacy K, Lisa N, Lynn P, Maggie K, Nancy S, Roberta B, Roni W, Sara B, Susan S, Tamara B + family, and Tom D.

All of the beautiful community members who are hosting Love List Parties (like Tupperware parties, but with less plastic and more heart!) to promote this book.

Hidden Villa, home of Josephine's Cabin, a one-room retreat that has provided some essential ingredients—solitude, intention, and a little bit of magic.

My mother, whose everyday gifts of kindness and love (including giving cookies to the homeless and sending embroidered towels to my friends) have inspired me to find the joy in simple things throughout my entire life.

And to anyone else who I regrettably forgot to mention... thank you, too!

Thank you for being part of my life's work.

FAREWELL VIDEO

Dear reader,

Now that you've reached the very end of this book, I have one last surprise for you! It's a farewell video from me where I share a few final thoughts with you.

Scan the QR code below (or click the link) to watch.

Farewell for now...but not forever! I hope we'll stay connected online, perhaps through my blog, newsletter, videos, classes, and more.

Thank for you making space in your life to read this book—and to express what's in your heart to the people you love most.

QR Code

Farewell from Sherry!
simplycelebrate.net/see-you-again-soon